The Chefs of Hilton Head

Compiled by
John S. Colquhoun

Southern Islands Publishing
Beaufort, South Carolina

Acknowledgements

The cover design is from an original watercolor by Savannah, Georgia artist Ray Ellis.

Southern Islands Publishing would like to thank Faith Nance, Watermark Inc., Birmingham, Alabama and Nancy Buscher, Buscher Enterprizes, Charleston, South Carolina for their time and contributions.

All bases used in this book are Minor's products, courtesy of Heidi and David Sievers, owners of All Serve Inc. and distributors of Minor's bases.

Old Bay® seasonings, courtesy of McCormick Spices, Hunt Valley, Maryland.

Tabasco pepper sauce, courtesy of Paul McIlhenny, The McIlhenny Co., Avery Island, Louisiana.

Contents

Introduction

This collection of prized recipes is from some of the finest restaurants on Hilton Head Island. Over five years of interviewing the most talented chefs on the island have gone into this compilation. Over the years a number of the restaurants have made changes, thus some of the chefs identified here have moved on to other positions. But recipes, like good wine, withstand the passing of time. The publication of these personal favorites is intended to prolong the memories of those of us who have enjoyed the island's cuisine through the years.

My wish is for you to enjoy as many of these creations as possible in your own home.

John Colquhoun

SOUPS

Brie Soup

Peel coating off of the brie. Add to the chicken stock. Bring to a boil. Add the cream and reduce to desired thickness. Garnish with the nutmeg and the Granny Smith apple.

SERVES 6

4 ounces Brie wheel
1 quart chicken stock
2 cups whipping cream
pinch of nutmeg
1 Granny Smith apple, diced

Chef Thierry Saglier,
Harbour Lights Bakery

3 tablespoons unsalted
  butter
2 cups yellow onions,
  sliced
2 cups leeks, sliced
2/3 cup scallions, sliced
1/3 cup shallots,
  minced
1 1/2 tablespoons
  garlic, minced
1 1/2 tablespoons flour
7 cups chicken stock
pinch of cayenne
  pepper
1 cup cognac
1 1/2 tablespoons
  lemon juice
2 tablespoons ginger,
  minced
salt to taste
fresh ground black
  pepper to taste

Four Onion Soup

Heat the butter. Add the onions, leeks, scallions, shallots and garlic. Sauté until golden brown then add the flour. Mix well and brown slightly. Add the stock and the next 5 ingredients. Bring to a boil. Simmer for 30 minutes. Add the ginger and adjust seasonings to taste.
SERVES 10

Chef Michael Sigler,
The Westin Resort

Gazpacho Europa

In a food processor, finely chop the cucumbers, pepper and onion. Remove to a large mixing bowl.

Add all of the remaining ingredients and stir thoroughly. Chill for at least 4 hours.

Adjust the seasonings if desired. If too thick add more tomato juice.

SERVES 8

3 cucumbers, peeled
1 large green pepper, seeded
1 large yellow onion, peeled
3 large zucchini, diced
4 cups tomatoes, finely chopped
1 quart tomato juice
1/4 cup red wine vinegar
2 teaspoons salt
1 teaspoon garlic, minced
3 tablespoons lime juice
2 tablespoons Worcestershire sauce
1 tablespoon Tabasco pepper sauce

Courtesy of Bev & Lou Gerber,
Café Europa

Hot and Sour Soup

1/4 cup carrots, sliced

1 to 1 1/2 ounces corn starch

1 egg

1/4 cup leeks, chopped

1/4 cup shiitake mushrooms, sliced

1/4 cup scallions

1/4 cup red bell peppers, diced

1 cup white radishes, diced

1/2 tablespoon water

3 quarts chicken stock

1 to 1 1/2 teaspoons sesame oil (heated)

1/2 teaspoon garlic, minced

4 tablespoons soy sauce

6 tablespoons white vinegar

8 ounces chicken breast

Skin the chicken breast, trimming the fat away. Poach the chicken breast in the chicken stock for approximately 7 minutes. Let stand at room temperature until cool. Julienne* into 1/2" pieces. Bring the stock to a medium boil. Add the carrots, leeks, radishes, red pepper, soy sauce and garlic. Reduce heat to a low boil and add the chicken. Mix the water and cornstarch together and add to the soup. Cook for 5 minutes. Reduce heat and add the egg, stirring only once. Add the mushrooms, scallions, vinegar and hot sesame oil. Let stand 5 minutes on low heat, stirring lightly. Taste and adjust the seasoning as needed with salt and pepper.

SERVES 8

*See glossary.

*Chef Steve Felenczak,
Hyatt Regency*

Manhattan Clam Chowder

In a 3-gallon stock pot, add the oil, heat and sauté the celery and onions until clear. Add the dry spices, then the clams and clam juice. Put in the remaining ingredients except the carrots and potatoes. Bring to boil, and simmer for 1 hour. Add the carrots and potatoes. Cook until the carrots and potatoes are tender.
SERVES 50

Chef Thomas J. Miller,
Café at Wexford

1 1/2 bunches celery, diced
1 1/2 large onions, diced
1 tablespoon basil, finely chopped
1 tablespoon thyme, finely chopped
1 tablespoon pepper
1 tablespoon red pepper
clam juice
1 gallon clams, chopped
6 tomatoes, diced
6 large potatoes, diced
3 cups tomato paste
1/2 cup lemon juice
1/4 cup Worcestershire sauce
1/4 cup red wine vinegar
1/4 cup port or burgundy wine
12 ounces clam base,* optional
1/2 cup oil
* See glossary.

She-Crab Soup

1 cup butter

2 tablespoons onions, diced

2 teaspoons celery, diced

1 1/2 tablepoons flour

*3 tablespoons Minor's lobster base**

1 quart milk

1 pint cream

1/4 teaspoon white pepper

1 pound white crab meat

2 tablespoons cream sherry

** See glossary.*

Melt the butter in a heavy saucepan. Sauté the onion and celery until soft, but not brown. Blend in the flour until smooth. Blend in the lobster base. Add the milk, gradually. Stirring constantly add the cream and white pepper. Cook slowly until hot, then add the crabmeat. When hot and slightly thickened, add the sherry to taste.
SERVES 6

*Chef Tom Oliva,
Crazy Crab, Harbour Town*

SALADS

Artichoke Salad

Make a court bouillon* and cook the scallops. Cool immediately. Add the remaining ingredients with the scallops to a mixing bowl. Toss and refrigerate. Serve on a shell dish garnished with leaf lettuce.
SERVES 20

* See glossary.

Chef Robert C. Montbleau,
Port Royal Plantation Clubhouse

3/4 pound scallops
8 red peppers, julienned*
2 white onions,
   julienned*
1 yellow pepper,
   julienned*
3 red onions,
   julienned*
4 large tomatoes, diced
50 Greek olives
1 bunch parsley
   (optional)
1 bunch basil
5, 10-ounce cans
   artichoke hearts,
   halved
1/2 cup garlic, minced
1 bunch tarragon
3 tablespoons red
   pepper, crushed
2 tablespoons salt
juice of 2 lemons
1/2 cup vermouth
3 tablespoons black
   pepper
1/2 cup olive oil
pinch of saffron
*See glossary.

Creamy Garlic and Herb Salad Dressing

8 cups mayonnaise
1/2 cup vinegar
2 tablespoons
 Parmesan cheese,
 grated
1/2 teaspoon sweet
 basil
1/2 teaspoon thyme
1/2 teaspoon oregano
1/2 teaspoon black
 pepper
4 1/2 teaspoons garlic
 powder
3 cups milk

Combine all of the ingredients in a large mixing bowl. Mix until well blended. Let stand for about 15 minutes. Taste and adjust the seasoning if necessary. The dressing may thicken as it sets. Thin it down with milk, if desired.

YIELDS 3 QUARTS

Chef Michael J. Zornouski,
The Westin Resort

Curried Chicken Salad

In a large bowl, combine the chicken, cashews, celery, green onion, apple and raisins. Blend the chutney, mayonnaise, curry and lemon juice and combine with the chicken mixture. Season to taste with the cayenne and garlic salt. Add additional curry if desired. Chill.

Serve in the prepared melon halves and garnish with a small bunch of green grapes.
SERVES 4

Note: The above measurement of curry is fairly mild. Flamingo's adds somewhat more when preparing the recipe at the restaurant.

Chef Deborah Van Plew,
Flamingo's Café

3 cups cold, poached
  chicken, shredded
1/2 cup cashews,
  coarsely chopped
2 stems celery, diced
2 tablespoons green
  onion, chopped
1 green apple, cored
  and diced
2 tablespoons raisins
2 teaspoons chutney
3/4 - 1 cup mayonnaise
2 teaspoons curry
  powder
2 teaspoons lemon
  juice
cayenne pepper to
  taste
garlic salt to taste
2 cantaloupes, halved,
  seeded and fluted*
bunch of green grapes

* See glossary.

2 tablespoons oil
1 tablespoon white
vinegar
2 teaspoons fresh dill
6 tablespoons whipping
cream
salt to taste
1 cup shiitake or
Golden Oak
mushrooms
1/4 bunch fresh
watercress
fresh ground black
pepper to taste

Dilled Mushroom and Watercress Salad

Mix together the oil, vinegar, dill, cream, salt and pepper. Add the mushrooms and toss. Place the bed of watercress on a large salad plate and top with the mushroom mixture. Garnish with fresh ground pepper.
SERVES 2

Chef Thierry Saglier,
Harbour Lights Bakery

English Stilton with Walnut Salad

Slice the radicchio and romaine lettuce into julienne* strips. The spinach and endive should remain in whole leaves. Coarsely chop the walnuts and crumble the Stilton cheese. Lay the spinach and endive leaves (3 per portion), on each serving plate. Arrange the other ingredients on top. Mix all of the ingredients for the dressing and serve over the top of the salad.
SERVES 4

*See glossary.

Chef Gerard Thompson,
Windows on Harbour Town

*1 head radicchio lettuce**
1/2 head romaine lettuce
2 ounces spinach
1 head endive
8 tablespoons walnuts
4 tablespoons Stilton cheese
8 yellow pear tomatoes, cut into wedges

Dressing:
6 tablespoons balsamic vinegar
5/8 cup walnut oil
1 teaspoon parsley, chopped
1 teaspoon red onion, finely diced
1 teaspoon watercress, chopped
1 teaspoon salt and pepper
1/2 teaspoon garlic, chopped

** See glossary.*

3 to 4 heads baby
lettuce
1/4 pound wild
mushrooms
2 tablespoons oil
50 shrimp, peeled and
deveined
1 bulb fennel,
julienned*
3 large leeks,
julienned*
1 large carrot,
julienned*
1 large onion,
julienned*
salt and pepper to
taste

Vinaigrette:
1 clove garlic, chopped
12 basil leaves,
chopped
1 large tomato, peeled,
seeded and diced
juice of 1 lemon
1 cup peanut oil
seasonings to taste
*See glossary

Sautéed Shrimp and Steamed Vegetable Salad

Clean the lettuce and wild mushrooms, then set aside. Heat the oil in a large sauté pan. Add the shrimp and season to taste. Sauté the shrimp until pink and firm. Remove and set aside. Steam the julienned vegetables and wild mushrooms for 3 to 5 minutes. Remove from the steamer and allow to cool.

Whisk together the garlic, basil, tomato and lemon juice in a bowl. Slowly whisk in the peanut oil and season to taste. Arrange the lettuce on a serving plate and place the steamed vegetables in the center. Top with the shrimp and lace with the vinaigrette.
SERVES 10-12

*Chef Jim McLain,
formerly of Wexford Plantation,
currently of Callawassie Island*

APPETIZERS

Artichoke Hearts and Crabmeat Sauté

Melt the butter and add the artichoke hearts, crabmeat, lemon juice, vermouth and shallots. Bring to a boil for one minute. Add the parsley and scallions.

Place the artichoke mixture over the spinach and serve.

SERVES 4

1/2 stick butter
10-ounce can artichoke hearts, chopped
8 ounces fresh crabmeat
3 tablespoons lemon juice
2 tablespoons vermouth
1 tablespoon shallots, minced
2 tablespoons parsley, chopped
2 tablespoons scallions, minced
1/2 bag of spinach, washed & shredded

Chef Johnny Highberger,
High Z's

Artichoke Heart Fritters

20 artichoke hearts
1 egg
pinch of sugar
pinch of salt
pinch of pepper
4 tablespoons cream
2 ounces water
2 ounces beer
1 cup flour
2 cups oil

Wash and clean the artichoke hearts and pat dry with a towel. Set aside. Combine the egg and the following six ingredients. Blend with a wire whisk until the batter starts to thicken. Adjust the thickness by adding water slowly. Do not over dilute.

Dredge the artichoke hearts in the flour and place in the batter, coating thoroughly. Heat the oil in a heavy skillet. Place the fritters in the oil and cook all sides approximately 3 minutes or until golden brown. Remove and pat dry with a towel. Season with salt and pepper.

SERVES 4

Chef Geoffrey Fennessey,
La Pola's

Carolina Bayou Smoked Gator Stuffed Shrimp

Combine the basil, butter and honey for the marinade and glaze the gatormeat while warming the smoker. Then smoke for 3 to 5 minutes. Allow the meat to cool.

Peel, devein and butterfly the shrimp, leaving the tails on. Sprinkle lightly with the "Old Bay Seasoning" and butter.

Remove all of the cartilage from the crabmeat. Grind the gatormeat and crabmeat to a hamburger consistency and set aside. Combine all of the remaining ingredients and sauté until soft. Drain and add to the gator and crabmeat mixture. Stuff the shrimp with the filling and dust lightly with the flour. Bake at 375° for 8 to 10 minutes.
SERVES 100

*Chef Gary D. Williams,
formerly of Long Cove Club,
currently of Captain's Seafood*

2 pounds gator tail
   meat
1 stick butter
1/4 cup basil, chopped
1 cup honey
5 pounds (51-60
   count shrimp)
1 pound lump
   crabmeat
6 cups saltine crackers,
   crushed fine
3 cups flour
8 eggs
6 medium shallots,
   minced
1/2 cup brandy
1/2 stalk celery, minced
2 medium carrots, diced
1 large onion, diced
salt and pepper
Tabasco pepper sauce
4 tablespoons
   Worcestershire sauce
1 cup heavy cream
"Old Bay Seasoning"*
butter
*See glossary.

Carolina Seafood Biscuits with Pernod

*2 regular size sheets
   puff pastry dough
1/4 cup flour
1 small bunch parsley,
   finely chopped
4-6 large shrimp
4-6 large scallops
1, 6-ounce lobster tail,
   shelled
1 stick butter
1/4 cup dry white
   wine
1 egg (for egg wash)
1 to 1 1/2 cups heavy
   cream
roux*
dash of Pernod
salt and pepper
pinch of dill*

** See glossary.*

Thaw the puff pastry at room temperature. Place on a lightly floured surface and sprinkle on the chopped parsley. Cut 24 circles out of the dough using a medium cookie cutter.

Cut the seafood into small pieces. Preheat the sauté pan. Add the butter, then the seafood and white wine. Sauté for 2-3 minutes. Salt and pepper to taste. Place the seafood on the circles of dough. Top each with another circle of dough and seal it with an egg wash. Bake at 350° until brown.

Meanwhile, in a saucepan, mix the leftover juice from the seafood with the cream, and bring to a boil. Make a roux from the remainder of the flour and butter. Salt and pepper to taste. Thin with the cream mixture. Add the Pernod for flavor and the dill for color. Spoon the sauce over the biscuits and serve.

SERVES 4

*Chef Gary D. Williams,
formerly of Long Cove Club,
currently of Captain's Seafood*

Chèvre Stuffed Mushrooms

Clean the mushrooms, separating the caps and stems. Set the caps aside. Chop the following into small pieces: mushroom stems, onion, green pepper and red pepper. In a large skillet, sauté the chopped vegetables and the garlic in olive oil. Add the fennel seed and crumbled bacon. Continue to sauté until the vegetables are tender. Remove from the heat. Fold in the chèvre cheese and the Parmesan cheese. Let the mixture stand for at least one hour to combine the flavors. Stuff the mushroom caps with the cheese mixture and broil until the caps are tender.

YIELDS 3 DOZEN

3 dozen large mushrooms
1 small onion
1 green pepper
1 red pepper
2 tablespoons olive oil
1 teaspoon garlic, minced
1 1/2 tablespoons fennel seed
3/4 cup bacon, cooked and crumbled
12 ounces chèvre cheese*
1/4 cup Parmesan cheese, grated

* See glossary.

*Chef Scott Miller,
Charlie's*

*1 pound bacon, finely
    diced*
1 onion, finely diced
1 whole pimento, diced
salt and pepper
*24 raw clams in their
    shells*

Clams Casino

Sauté the bacon and the onions until the bacon is crisp and the onions are translucent. Drain off the grease, and add the pimento. Season with the salt and pepper. Open the clams. Place 6 clams on the half shell on a sheet pan. Divide the casino mix evenly and place on top of each clam. Sprinkle with butter and bake 8 - 10 minutes at 350°.
SERVES 6

*Chef Robert Montbleau,
Port Royal Plantation Clubhouse*

Country Paté

Grind finely the following: 2 pounds of pork meat, pork liver, garlic, onion, and parsley. Grind the remaining meat coarsely. Place all of the ingredients in a mixing bowl, beat slowly, adding the flour, eggs, seasoning, brandy and heavy cream. Place the mixture in a terrine.* Cook in a water bath* in a 325° oven until done.

Refrigerate overnight. Serve with thin slices of warm toast and garnish with cornichons.*
YIELDS 10 - 12 slices

* See glossary.

5 pound boneless pork butt
1 pound pork liver
3-4 garlic cloves
1/2 pound onions
5 sprigs parsley
5 ounces flour
4 eggs
1 ounce salt
pinch of curing salt
1/2 teaspoon ground pepper
2 tablespoons brandy
1/2 pint heavy cream

Chef Geoffrey Fennessey,
La Pola's

Crab Cakes

1 pound lump
crabmeat
1/2 teaspoon dry
mustard
3 teaspoons lemon
juice
1 tablespoon parsley,
chopped
1 teaspoon garlic,
chopped
1/4 teaspoon salt
1 teaspoon
Worcestershire sauce
1/4 teaspoon Tabasco
pepper sauce
2 eggs
2 tablespoons heavy
cream
1/4 cup crackers,
crumbled
vegetable oil
fresh lemon wedges

Clean the crabmeat of any shells and place in a mixing bowl. Add the mustard, lemon, parsley, garlic, salt, Worcestershire and Tabasco sauces to the crabmeat and mix. Add the eggs, cream and half of the cracker crumbs. Mix gently. Adjust the seasoning to taste. Form into 3-ounce patties and pat remaining broken crumbs on the outside. Sauté the cakes in oil or deep fry until golden brown. Serve with fresh lemon.

SERVES 4 - 6

Chef Robert A. Fedorko,
The Westin Resort

Crab Stuffed Mushrooms

Heat the butter and sauté the garlic and shallots on low heat for 3 minutes. Add the flour, cooking and stirring for 2 minutes. Blend in the cream and stir with a whisk, cooking one minute, until thick and creamy. Slowly stir in the wine. Add the Ritz crackers, crabmeat, salt, pepper and lemon juice. Mix well. Set aside to cool.

Clean the mushrooms, removing the stems. Spoon the crab stuffing into the mushroom caps. Place in a shallow baking dish and bake for 20 minutes. Just before serving, top with a hollandaise or bearnaise sauce.

SERVES 6 - 8

1/4 stick butter
1 teaspoon garlic, finely chopped
1 teaspoon shallots, finely chopped
4 tablespoons all-purpose flour
1/2 cup heavy cream
1/2 cup dry white wine
1 cup crackers, ground
1/2 pound white crab meat
1/2 teaspoon salt
1/2 tablespoon white pepper
2 tablespoons lemon juice
20 large fresh mushrooms

Chef Tom Oliva,
Crazy Crab, Harbour Town

Easy Cheese Soufflé

4 tablespoons butter
4 tablespoons flour
11 ounces milk
6 egg yolks
7 egg whites
4 ounces Gruyère
  cheese, grated
4 tablespoons
  Parmesan cheese
salt and pepper

Melt the butter in a saucepan, adding the flour. Boil the milk and add to the flour mixture. Grease an 8" soufflé dish and dust with the flour or grated Parmesan cheese. Preheat the oven to 375°. Incorporate the egg yolks one by one, mixing well after each addition. Add the cheese and season to taste. Beat the egg whites to a stiff peak. Fold carefully into the cheese mixture. Fill the soufflé dish to 1" under the rim and bake for 35 minutes. SERVES 2

Chef Geoffory Fennessey,
La Pola's

Escargots in Phyllo Dough

Defrost the phyllo dough as directed on the package. Rinse the escargots under cold water and pat dry with paper towels. Lay out the phyllo dough on plastic wrap and brush both sides with the melted butter. Place the sheets of dough together evenly. Cut the dough into 12 even squares. Place 1 tablespoon of Boursin cheese in the center of each square and place 1 escargot on top of the cheese. Draw up all the sides of the dough to form a small sachet. These will hold together un-cooked for 24 hours in the refrigerator. Place each sachet on a greased baking sheet. Bake at 375° until golden brown. Serve hot from the oven.
SERVES 2

2 phyllo dough sheets
12 escargots
6 ounces Boursin cheese
3 tablespoons butter, melted

Chef Robert A. Fedorko,
The Westin Resort

Hush Puppies

2 cups self-rising flour
2 cups corn meal
2 1/2 cups buttermilk
 or whole milk
1 cup mayonnaise
1 teaspoon Tabasco
 pepper sauce
1/2 cup sugar
2 cups onions, diced
1 teaspoon salt
1 teaspoon pepper
vegetable oil

In a large bowl, mix all of the dry ingredients with the milk, mayonnaise and Tabasco. Add the remaining ingredients, except the oil. Mix well and let stand for 30 minutes in the refrigerator.

Place 1 1/2 to 2 inches of oil in a deep fry pan and preheat to 350°. Using a 2 tablespoon scoop, drop the batter just above the hot oil to avoid any splatters. Cook 2 - 3 minutes or until golden. Drain well.

YIELD: 64 hush puppies, approximately.

Chef Tom Oliva,
Crazy Crab, Harbour Town

Jumbo Shrimp in Whole Grain Mustard Sauce

Peel and devein the shrimp leaving the tails on. Sauté the shrimp in the clarified butter. Remove the shrimp and deglaze* the pan with the sherry. Add the shallots and the cream. Reduce to the desired thickness. Add the mustard and adjust the seasoning.

Serve the shrimp with an angel hair pasta, tossed in butter.

SERVES 1

* See glossary.

*Chef Michael Sigler,
The Westin Resort*

*5 jumbo shrimp
2 tablespoons clarified
  butter*
1/4 cup sherry
1 teaspoon shallots
1/2 cup cream
salt and pepper to taste
1 teaspoon whole grain
  mustard*

* See glossary.*

16 plump oysters
1/2 cup peanut oil
3/4 cup all-purpose
 flour
6 large eggs, beaten

Hollandaise Sauce:
4 egg yolks
2 tablespoons water
10 ounces clarified
 butter*
2 tablespoons lemon
 juice
pinch of salt and
 pepper
5 drops Tabasco
 pepper sauce
1 tablespoon fresh dill,
 chopped

* See glossary.

Oysters Anna with Dill Hollandaise

Heat the oil in a frying pan. Dredge the oysters in flour, then immerse them into the beaten eggs and drop immediately into the hot oil. Turn once very gently. Drain on paper towels and keep warm.

To prepare the hollandaise sauce, place the egg yolks and water in the top part of a simmering double boiler. Beat vigorously with a whisk until the eggs are the consistency of condensed milk. Stirring constantly, slowly add the clarifed butter. Add the lemon juice, salt and pepper, Tabasco and dill.

Ladle the hollandaise sauce onto a serving platter and place the oysters on top of the sauce. Sprinkle with the dill or caviar. Serve immediately.
SERVES 4

*Courtesy of Bev & Lou Gerber,
Café Europa*

Oysters Kilpatrick

Chop the bacon and sauté until brown. Add the onion, garlic, "Season-All" and tomatoes. Sauté until the onions are transparent. Cool for 20 minutes. Add the bread crumbs. Salt and pepper to taste. Place 1-2 tablespoons of mixture on each oyster and bake until breading is light brown. Serve immediately.
SERVES 8 - 10

6 ounces bacon
1 medium onion, diced
2 tablespoons garlic, minced
3 teaspoons "Season-All"*
4 tomatoes, peeled and finely chopped
6 cups bread crumbs
3-5 dozen oysters, shucked
salt and pepper

See glossary.

Chef Geoffrey Fennessey,
La Pola's

Oysters "Port Royal"

*4 plump oysters in
season
1 tablespoon julienne
of smoked salmon
2 tablespoons lump
crabmeat
1 tablespoon butter
1/4 bunch parsley,
deep fried and salted*

Find the best oysters for the time of year and shuck. Top with the salmon, crab and butter. Warm in a 250° oven until the edges of the oysters just curl. Top with your favorite sauce, such as a bearnaise or mornay and broil until golden brown. Serve with lemon and the parsley.
YIELDS 4

*Chef Michael Zornouski,
The Westin Resort*

Pinckney Island Salsa

Mix all of the vegetables, herbs and spices, then add the corn oil, vinegar, Worcestershire and Tabasco sauces. Allow to marinate overnight to extract the vegetable juices. Blend in the tomato paste to thicken.

YIELDS 1 GALLON

1 onion, diced
1/2 stalk celery, diced
1/2 jalapeno pepper, minced
1 1/2 green bell peppers, diced
10 plum tomatoes, diced
1 1/2 tablespoons garlic, minced
1/2 cup cilantro, chopped
1/2 teaspoon cumin, ground
1/2 teaspoon salt
1/2 cup corn oil
1/4 cup red wine vinegar
1 1/2 tablespoons Worcestershire sauce
1 1/2 shakes Tabasco pepper sauce
1/2 cup tomato paste

Chef Dean A. Thomas,
The Westin Resort

Romaine, Wild Mushroom and Garlic Chive Torte

Lining:
*1/2 stick unsalted
   butter*
12-14 romaine leaves

Filling:
finely chopped:
   *1/2 pound
      mushrooms*
   2 stalks celery
   1/2 large onion
   *1 1/2 tablespoons
      fresh basil*
   *1 1/2 tablespoons of
      garlic chives*
4 tablespoons oil
1/2 cup sherry

Custard:
4 cups milk, scalded
*12 whole eggs, well
   beaten*
1 teaspoon nutmeg
*4 teaspoons parsley,
   chopped*

Butter the entire inside surface of a 9" cheesecake pan. Blanch the romaine leaves for a few seconds in hot water, then cool. Remove the middle stem from the leaves. Line the pan with the leaves and set aside.

To prepare the filling, combine all of the ingredients (except the sherry) and sauté for about 10 minutes. Add the sherry and cook until most of the liquid is gone. Season to taste and set aside.

Prepare the custard by bringing the milk to a boil. In a bowl combine the remaining ingredients. Whisk until well blended. Whisking continually, slowly add the scalded milk to the egg mixture.

(continued on the next page)

45

Sauce:
  6 medium red bell
    peppers
  3 cups water
  1 large onion
  3 tablespoons oil

By hand, combine the filling with the custard until well blended. Pour into the lined pan. Set the lined pan in a sheet pan half filled with water and bake at 400° for 30-45 minutes.

Prepare the sauce while the torte is cooling. Core, seed, and coarsely chop the bell peppers and boil until soft, then strain. Peel and slice the onion and sauté in the oil until soft. Purée the strained bell peppers with the onion in a food processor until smooth. Strain the puree and season to taste. Pour the sauce onto the plate and place the torte on the sauce and garnish as desired.
SERVES 6

Chef Jim McLain,
formerly of Wexford Plantation,
currently of Callawassie Island

16 jumbo shrimp
3/4 cup olive oil
1 teaspoon garlic,
    chopped
1/4 cup soy sauce
2 tablespoons sherry
4 tablespoons ketchup
pinch of oregano
pinch of dried basil
pinch of salt and
    pepper
4, 6" wooden skewers
1/2 stick butter,
    melted

Scampi Griglia Pescatora

Prepare the marinade in a shallow pan. Combine the olive oil, garlic, soy sauce, sherry, ketchup, oregano, basil, salt and pepper.

Split the shrimp from the bottom keeping the shell intact. Place four shrimp onto each skewer and marinate for 2 hours.

Grill on a charcoal grill while brushing with butter. The shells will burn slightly giving the shrimp a roasted flavor.

SERVES 4

Courtesy of Bev & Lou Gerber,
Café Europa

Shrimp Madagascar

Peel and devein the shrimp. Season with the salt and pepper. In a mixing bowl, combine the arrowroot, heavy cream and sour cream. Heat the sauté pan with the oil. Add the shrimp and crushed peppercorns. Sauté for 2 minutes. Flip the shrimp. Add Pernod and flambé. When the flame is extinguished, add the onions and cream mixture. Cook for 3 minutes. Season with the salt and pepper when the sauce is thickened. Serve immediately.
SERVES 4

2 pounds jumbo shrimp
salt and pepper
1 tablespoon arrowroot or cornstarch
1 cup heavy cream
1 cup sour cream
4 tablespoons oil
4 tablespoons crushed green peppercorns
3/4 cup Pernod
1 bunch green onions, sliced

Chef Scott Sundermeyer,
Hemingway's, Hyatt Regency

Shrimp Mousse

*1, 11-ounce can tomato
soup, undiluted
1/4 cup water
1 package unflavored
gelatin
8 ounces cream cheese
1 cup mayonnaise
1/2 cup celery, diced
1/2 cup onions, diced
1/2 cup green peppers,
diced
4 1/2 ounces cooked
shrimp, finely
chopped*

Heat the tomato soup until bubbling. Combine the gelatin and the water. Add to the soup and mix. Beat the cream cheese and mayonnaise until smooth. Add to the soup mixure, along with the celery, onion and green pepper. Fold in the shrimp, mixing thoroughly. Pour into a mold. Chill until set.
SERVES 6

*Chef Deborah Van Plew,
Flamingo's Café*

Spinach Linguini with Mussels

In a pot, bring water to a boil. Cook the pasta 8 - 10 minutes (do not overcook.) Strain and cool with water. In a sauté pan melt half of the butter in the olive oil. Combine all of the ingredients, except the cheese and heat slowly. When hot, add the cheese and remaining butter, then pour over the pasta. Put the pasta on the plate first, arranging the mussels as garnish.

SERVES 4

1 pound spinach
 linguini
20 mussels
2 tablespoons salt
3 quarts water
4 tablespoons butter
3 tablespoons olive oil
1/4 pound prosciutto
 ham, sliced very thin
1/2 cup toasted pine
 nuts
1 tablespoon shallots,
 minced
1 tablespoon fresh
 garlic, chopped
fresh ground pepper
1 1/2 to 2 cups fresh
 Parmesan cheese,
 grated

Chef Thomas J. Miller,
Café at Wexford

Steak Tartare

*6 ounce tenderloin
steak
1 teaspoon Dijon
mustard
1/2 teaspoon shallots,
chopped
1/4 teaspoon garlic,
chopped
1/2 teaspoon parsley,
chopped
1 anchovy filet, minced
1 egg yolk
1/2 teaspoon cognac
salt and pepper to taste
1 teaspoon capers
1/8 teaspoon paprika
1 tomato
1/2 onion, thinly sliced
2 slices bread
butter*

Chop the steak, while adding all of the next 10 ingredients until the meat is finely chopped and the ingredients are thoroughly mixed.

Serve well chilled on a plate garnished with tomato quarters, sliced raw onion, and bread and butter.

SERVES 2

*Courtesy Bev & Lou Gerber,
Café Europa*

ENTREES

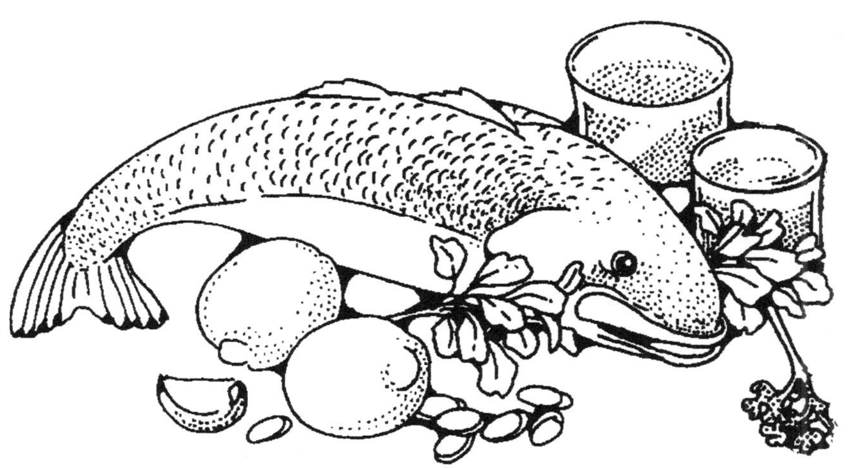

Asparagus with Oyster Mousseline Sauce

Peel all of the woody material from the asparagus. Open and strain the oysters. Save the liquid in a heavy saucepan. Cut the oysters into 1/8" strips. Set aside.

Heat the oyster liquid and add the wine. Heat to a boil and reduce by half. While the liquid is boiling, cook the asparagus 10 minutes in lightly salted boiling water. Remove from the heat but keep the asparagus in the water to stay warm.

Beat the egg yolks with a 1/2 cup of the asparagus liquid. Add this mixture to the oyster liquid-wine reduction. Whisk over a low heat until foamy and lightly thickened. Add the sliced oysters. Over a low heat, whisk in the heavy cream, butter and cayenne. Salt and pepper to taste. Drain the asparagus. Arrange and coat with the sauce.
SERVES 4

Chef Dave Plemmons,
Renaissance

24 asparagus spears, cut to 4" in length
8 - 12 oysters, with liquid
1/4 cup white table wine
4 egg yolks
2 tablespoons heavy cream
3 tablespoons butter
pinch of cayenne pepper
salt and pepper

1 medium eggplant, peeled and cut lengthwise into 1" strips

1 pound zucchini, rimmed and cut lengthwise into 1/4" slices

salt

12 spinach lasagna noodles

15 ounces Ricotta cheese

1/2 cup fresh basil, chopped

7 tablespoons grated parmesan cheese

1/8 teaspoon ground black pepper

6 tablespoons olive oil

1 large green bell pepper, chopped

1 large red bell pepper, chopped

1 large onion, halved and cut into long slices

(continued on next page)

Autumn Lasagna

Salt the eggplant and the zucchini and place between layers of paper towel. Top with a double layer of paper. Place a heavy (5 pound) tray on the top and press for 1 hour.

Cook the noodles in boiling, salted water until al dente and drain. Place the noodles in a large bowl of cool water. Mix the ricotta, half of the basil, 2 tablespoons of the Parmesan and the black pepper until blended.

Heat 2 tablespoons of oil in a large skillet. Add the peppers, onion and garlic. Cook, covered over a low heat, stirring occasionally until the peppers are tender. Uncover and sauté over a medium heat until the edges begin to brown. Stir in the corn, olives and the remaining basil. Season and set aside.

Squeeze the eggplant and the zucchini tightly in fresh paper towel to extract as much moisture as possible. Heat 2 tablespoons of the oil in a large skillet and fry the eggplant, turning to brown evenly. Drain and add more oil to the dry skillet, 2 tablespoons at a time. Fry the remaining eggplant and zucchini.

(continued on next page)

Spoon a 1/2 cup of the tomatoes into a 9" x 13" baking dish. Lift the noodles from the water and dry carefully with a paper towel. Arrange a single layer of the noodles over the tomatoes. Add a layer of the eggplant and zucchini and half the corn mixture. Sprinkle with 1 cup of mozzarella and 2 tablepoons of Parmesan.

Arrange a second layer of noodles and top with the ricotta mixture, remaining eggplant and zucchini, sprinkled with 1 cup of mozzarella. Arrange a third layer of noodles with the remaining corn mixture, tomatoes spinkled with mozzarella and 3 tablespoons of Parmesan.

Bake at 350° until the cheese is bubbling and the edges are brown. Let stand 5 minutes before cutting and serving.

Variation:

Add one of the following: cooked/drained sweet Italian sausage, kielbasa, prosciutto, ground beef or veal.

SERVES 10 - 15

2 minced garlic cloves
1 cup corn kernels
1/4 cup chopped ripe
  black or green olives
2 cups chopped
  tomatoes
3 cups mozarella,
  grated

Chef Deborah Van Plew,
Flamingo's Café

*1 1/2 pounds Cobia**

2 medium cucumbers,
  peeled

3 plum tomatoes

1 medium onion

1 red pepper, seeded

1 green pepper, seeded

1 yellow pepper, seeded

5 tablespoons olive oil

2 tablespoons flour

2 tablespoons sugar

1/4 cup balsamic
  vinegar

salt and pepper

** See glossary.*

Baked Cobia with Warm Golden Relish

To prepare the relish, chop all of the vegetables in 1/4" pieces. Heat 3 tablespoons of oil in a medium pan set on high. Add the onions and cook until tender. Reduce the heat. Add the flour and stir. Add the remaining vegetables and stir. Add the sugar and the vinegar. Reduce the heat to low, cover, and cook for 20 minutes. Remove the cover and cook for approximately 25 minutes. Salt and pepper to taste. Keep warm while preparing the cobia.

To prepare the cobia, preheat the oven to 350°. Heat the remaining oil in a heavy pan on high. Place the fish, skin side up, in the pan and cook for 1 minute. Turn the fish. Place in the oven and cook 15 minutes. Top with the relish and serve.

SERVES 4 - 6

Chef Richard Canestrari,
Café at Wexford

Baked Wahoo with Cream Crabmeat Sauce

Sauté the onion in the butter. Add the cheese and the remaining ingredients except the crabmeat. Allow to simmer. Beat with a whisk until the sauce becomes smooth. Add the crabmeat. If necessary, adjust the consistency with any additional fish stock. Bake the fish 15-20 minutes at 350°. Remove to a plate and pour the sauce over the fish. SERVES 4

4, 6-8 ounce fillets of Wahoo*
2 teaspoons onion, finely chopped
1/4 stick butter
1 pound cream cheese
2 cups fish stock
1/4 cup white wine
1/4 teaspoon lemon juice
salt and pepper
1 cup lump crabmeat

* See glossary.

Chef Mark Christian,
William F. Pelican Restaurant

24 ounces sirloin tip

Marinade:
1/2 teaspoon curry
   powder
1 tablespoon lemon
   grass
2 tablespoons peanut oil
1/4 teaspoon garlic,
   chopped
1/4 teaspoon ginger,
   chopped
1 1/2 teaspoons chili
   garlic sauce
1 teaspoon soy sauce

Peanut Sauce:
1/4 cup peanuts raw,
   or peanut butter
1/2 teaspoon garlic
1/2 cup coconut milk
1/2 cup chicken stock
1 teaspoon soy sauce
1 teaspoon sugar
1 teaspoon red pepper,
   ground
1 bay leaf
salt to taste

Beef Satay

Combine all of the marinade ingredients in a large mixing bowl.

Cut the sirloin into 1/4" slices, 2" long. Coat with the marinade and skewer. Let stand overnight.

To prepare the peanut sauce, combine all of the ingredients in a saucepan over a moderate heat. Bring to a boil, then continue simmering until the sauce is thick. Adjust the seasonings, remove the bay leaf, and serve.

After the skewered sirloin strips have marinated, cook on a griddle for about 1 to 1 1/2 minutes each side.

Serve with the peanut sauce and steamed rice on the side. Garnish with pieces of scallion (5" long) and half a cherry tomato.
SERVES 4

Chef Steve Felenczak,
Hyatt Regency

Broiled Grouper with Crab Imperial Sauce

Sauté the onion, pepper, and pimento in a small amount of butter. When soft, add the cream, fish stock, wine, juice, salt and pepper. Allow to simmer, then add the crabmeat. Thicken with a roux* mixture of blended butter and flour adding slowly until the desired consistency is reached. Broil the grouper and top with the sauce.
SERVES 4

*See glossary.

4, 6-ounce grouper fillets
1/2 medium onion, diced
1/2 medium bell pepper, diced
2 teaspoons pimento, diced
1/2 cup butter
3 cups heavy cream
1 cup fish stock
1/4 cup white wine
2 tablespoons lemon juice
salt and pepper
1 cup lump crabmeat
flour

Chef Mark Christian,
William F. Pelican Restaurant

3/4 cup vegetable oil
1 cup all-purpose flour
1/2 cup celery, chopped
1 cup onions, chopped
1/2 cup green peppers,
* chopped*
2 tablespoons garlic,
* minced*
1/2 teaspoon cayenne
* pepper*
1 tablespoon oregano
1 tablespoon basil
1 pound chicken
* breast, cut into 1"*
* cubes*
1 cup kielbasa sausage,
* sliced*
1/2 pound raw shrimp
* with tails still on*
1 16-ounce can
* chicken broth*
2 cups cooked rice

Cajun Jambalaya

Heat a 1/2 cup of the oil in a heavy skillet until very hot. Whisk in the flour, stirring constantly until smooth and dark. Reduce the heat by half and simmer for 20 minutes. Add the vegetables, garlic and spices, cooking for 5 minutes. In a large pot, heat the chicken broth. Add the vegetable mixture and simmer for 20 minutes.

Sauté the chicken and sausage for 5 minutes in the remaining 1/4 cup of oil. Pour off the oil, add to the flour mixture and then add the shrimp. Cook on medium high heat until the sauce is bubbling.

Serve over rice.

SERVES 4

Chef Johnny Highberger,
High Z's

Carolina Swamp Bog Chili

Combine the sausage and the ground chuck with the finely diced celery and onion and sauté. After 2 minutes, add the garlic. Combine all of the powdered seasonings and the liquid smoke and add to the meat when cooked. Lightly precook the kidney beans and add to the meat mixture. Add the tomato paste and water to the meat mixture. Allow to simmer 3-5 hours.
YIELDS 1 GALLON

*Chef Gary D. Williams,
formerly of Long Cove Club,
currently of Captain's Seafood*

*1 pound ground chuck
1 pound Italian
    sausage
3-4 celery stalks
1 small onion
4 cloves of garlic, minced
1 tablespoon onion
    powder
2 tablespoons hickory
    flavored liquid
    smoke
2 tablespoons celery
    seed
1/4 cup salt
1 tablespoon white
    pepper
3 bay leaves
2 tablespoons cayenne
    pepper
1/4 cup Cajun seasoning
1/4 cup sugar
1/2 cup chili powder
1/2 pound red kidney
    beans
1, 6-ounce can tomato
    paste
1 1/2 cups water*

1 1/2 pounds tender-
    loin, finely sliced
1 fennel bulb
5 anchovy fillets,
    chopped
1/2 clove garlic
1/2 bunch parsley
1/4 cup olive oil
3 tablespoons red wine
    vinegar
1 tablespoon capers

Carpaccio and Fennel

Cut the tenderloin into 4, 6-ounce medal-lions. Pound the medallions until paper thin. Slice the fennel very thin and place in water. In a food processor, puree the anchovy, garlic, parsley, oil and vinegar. Place the fennel underneath the tenderloin and pour the purée over the top. Sprinkle the capers on the purée.
SERVES 4

Chef Alain Tiphaine,
Capt's Table

Chicken Alfredo

To prepare the sauce, combine the first four ingredients in a saucepan and whisk over medium heat until the cheese is blended. Add the Parmesan to the cream mixture and thicken with the roux or with cornstarch or by natural reduction.

In a sauté pan, heat the clarified butter and sauté the chicken and the onion. When the chicken is almost cooked, stir in the mushrooms and scallions. Continue cooking a few minutes before adding the sauce, then reduce the heat. Cut the tomatoes in half. Slightly blanch the broccoli. Add the tomatoes and broccoli to the sauté pan. Serve over the pasta.
SERVES 2.

Chef Jeff Hendrickson,
Sea Pines Plantation Club

Sauce:
4 ounces cream cheese
2 cups chicken stock*
2 teaspoons garlic
  powder
1/2 teaspoon white
  pepper
1/3 cup Parmesan
  cheese
roux**

2, 6-ounce chicken
  breasts, cut into
  chunks
2 tablespoons clarified
  butter**
1/3 cup diced onions
1 cup sliced mushrooms
1/4 cup minced
  scallions
6 cherry tomatoes
1/2 cup broccoli florets
cooked pasta

* 1, 16-ounce can of
chicken broth may be
substituted.
** See glossary.

Chicken Breast with Basil

1, 6-ounce skinless, boneless chicken breast
salt and pepper to taste
2 ounces ricotta cheese
4 fresh basil leaves
1 egg yolk

Season the chicken breasts with salt and pepper. Blend the cheese and add the finely chopped basil, salt and pepper. Add the egg yolk and mix thoroughly. Stuff the cheese mixture into the chicken breast. Roll and secure with toothpicks, and bake in a 300° oven for 30 minutes or until done.
SERVES 1

Chef Gerard Thompson,
Windows on Harbour Town

Chicken Crêpes with Rosemary Cream Sauce

Preheat oven to 450°. Sauté the onion in the butter and add the chicken base or bouillon. Whisk in the cream and milk and add the herbs. Thicken the sauce on a low heat until bubbly around the edge. Sauté the chicken until lightly browned. Cool slightly and cut into 1/4" strips.

Place 2 crêpes in each individual oblong casserole dish. Place chicken strips (equivalent to 1 breast) on the crêpes. Add enough of the cream sauce to cover the strips. Roll the crêpes around the filling and top with more cream sauce. Add the cheese to cover the surface of the casseroles and brown in the oven close to the heat.
SERVES 6

1/2 pound butter
1/2 cup onions, diced
1/2 teaspoon chicken
   base or 1/2 cup
   chicken bouillon
1 pint whipping cream
1 pint milk
1 1/2 teaspoons
   rosemary
1/2 teaspoon thyme
6 boneless chicken
   breasts, skinned
12 crêpe shells
1/2 cup Swiss or
   Gruyère cheese,
   shredded

Chef Deborah Van Plew,
Flamingo's Café

Chicken Veronique

*1 cup whipping
cream
2 cups mayonnaise
1 1/2 cups seedless,
green grapes
2 teaspoons
Worcestershire sauce
3 tablespoons Dijon
mustard
1 tablespoon lemon
juice
1/2 teaspoon Tabasco
pepper sauce
3 whole chicken
breasts, poached or
roasted and diced
2 cantaloupes*

Whip the cream until it holds stiff peaks. Fold into the mayonnaise. Wash and dry the grapes folding them and the next four ingredients into the cream mixture. Mix a desired amount of the dressing with the chicken. Serve in scallop-edged melon halves on a bed of lettuce.
SERVES 4

*Chef Chad Newman,
Charlie's*

Crabmeat Stuffing

Sauté the onions and celery in the butter until tender. Add the crabmeat, bay leaf, clam juice and sherry. Simmer for about 5 minutes. Add the Old Bay® seasoning and cayenne pepper. Cook the mixture until well blended. Remove from the heat and add the bread cubes and crackers. Mix well, then add the mustard and mayonnaise and let cool.

Excellent for stuffing flounder, grouper and trout.

SERVES 12

1 pound snow or lump crabmeat

10 tablespoons onion, coarsely chopped

6 tablespoons celery, coarsely chopped

3 tablespoons butter

1 bay leaf

3/4 cup clam juice

8 tablespoons cream sherry

1 teaspoon Old Bay® seasoning

cayenne pepper

1 cup plus 3 table- spoons cubed bread (1/2" cubes)

3 tablespoons crackers, crushed

1 tablespoon Dijon mustard

2 tablespoons mayon- naise

Chef Michael Zornouski,
The Westin Resort

Eggplant Parmigiano

4 eggplant slices
1/2 cup marinara
   sauce
4 tablespoons
   Parmesan cheese,
   grated
1/2 cup Mozzarella
   cheese, shredded
1/2 cup Ricotta cheese
parsley
4 tablespoons oil

Fry the eggplant in the oil until tender. Spoon 1 ounce of the marinara onto the bottom of a baking dish. Add two slices of the eggplant from the fryer. Add half of the Parmesan cheese, half of the mozzarella and all of the ricotta. Top with the remaining eggplant and cover with the marinara sauce. Add the remaining mozzarella and Parmesan cheese. Cook in a preheated 350° oven for 10 minutes. Garnish with two dots of marinara sauce and parsley.

SERVES 1

Chef Robert Montbleau,
Port Royal Plantation Clubhouse

Fillet of Flounder with Tomatoes and Chervil

Clean the flounder and slice into four portions. Peel and dice the tomatoes and mix with the chervil and cheese. In a buttered dish, spread the shallots, then add the flounder and tomatoes. Bake for 7 minutes in a 450° oven. Mix the white wine and cream. Boil for 4 minutes. Place the flounder mixture on a plate, top with the sauce, and serve.

SERVES 4

2, 8-ounce flounder fillets
4 tomatoes
1 bunch chervil*
5 ounces Swiss cheese, shredded
2 shallots, finely diced
1 1/4 cups white wine
1 pint cream
1/4 cup butter
salt and pepper

* Parsley can be substituted.

Chef Jean Loup Kunckler,
The Gaslight

Flounder Daufuskie

*4 whole flounders,
  boned and poached**
*1 pound crabmeat
  from claws***
1 green bell pepper
1 red bell pepper
1 onion
*8 oysters, shucked with
  liquid*
salt and pepper
fresh bread, cubed
1 stick butter
*sweet Hungarian
  paprika*

**To bone the flounder,
cut through the top
half of the flounder,
cut- ting out the spinal
bone with kitchen
shears at both top and
bottom. With a boning
knife, cut along the
cartilage and remove
the skeletal area.*
***Pick through crab
meat to remove shell
fragments.*

Dice the pepper and onion and boil for 4 minutes. Chop the oysters and mix with the crab, bread, cooled vegetables, salt and pepper. Add half of the butter, melted. Mix well. Stuff the flounder. Drizzle the remaining butter on top of the exposed mixture showing at the tip of the flounder. Sprinkle the paprika on top and bake for 20 minutes at 350°.
SERVES 4

*Courtesy of Bev & Lou Gerber,
Café Europa*

Flounder a l'orange

Heat the margarine in a large frying pan over medium-high heat. Get the margarine hot enough so that a small drop of beaten egg will bubble up immediately on contact.

Dredge the fillets in flour and shake off the excess. Dip the fillets in the beaten egg, and place in the pan, white sides down.

Cook for 2 minutes, carefully turn the fillets, and cook for 2 more minutes.

Add the Grand Marnier around the side of the pan, and ignite.

When the flame has died down, add the orange juice, butter and chopped parsley. Cook the sauce until it thickens to the desired consistency. Serve garnished with orange slices.
SERVES 4

4 tablespoons margarine
4, 8-ounce flounder fillets (white sides)
3 eggs, beaten with 1 tablespoon of water
2 cups flour
2 ounces Grand Marnier
1/2 cup orange juice
2 tablespoons butter
1 tablespoon parsley, chopped

Courtesy of Bev & Lou Gerber,
Café Europa

Flounder Mentonaise

4, 8-ounce flounder fillets (white sides down)
4 tablespoons margarine
3 eggs, beaten with 1 tablespoon of water
2 cups flour
1/4 cup Pernod
*1 small zucchini, julienned**
1 tomato, julienned
2 tablespoons butter
1 tablespoon parsley, chopped

**See glossary.*

Heat the margarine in a large frying pan over medium-high heat. Get the margarine hot enough so that a small drop of beaten egg will bubble up immediately on contact.

Dredge the fillets in flour and shake off the excess. Dip the fillets in the beaten egg and place in the pan, white sides down.

Cook for 2 minutes. Carefully turn the fillets and cook for 2 more minutes.

Add the Pernod around the side of the pan and ignite.

When the flame has died down, add the julienned zucchini and tomato, the butter, and chopped parsley. Allow the butter to melt, and the zucchini and tomato to wilt slightly.

Serve with the vegetables on top of the fillets.
SERVES 4

Courtesy of Bev & Lou Gerber, Café Europa

Fresh Scallops Provençale

Clean the scallops. Season with the salt and pepper and flour lightly. Heat the oil in a non-stick pan and cook the scallops until lightly brown. Remove from the pan and add garlic, parsley, tomatoes and thyme, cooking for 5 minutes. Add the butter and pour over the scallops. Serve with rice or boiled potatoes.

SERVES 4

1 1/2 pounds fresh scallops
salt, pepper, flour
2 tablespoons olive oil
3 cloves chopped garlic
1 1/2 tablespoons chopped parsley
2 medium tomatoes, diced
pinch of thyme
1 tablespoon soft butter

Chef Jean-Loup Kunckler,
The Gaslight

*4, 8-ounce chicken
breasts, skinned and
boned*

1 cup olive oil

*1/3 cup tarragon
vinegar*

*1 teaspoon herb/spice
mixture (oregano,
basil, salt, thyme,
garlic powder)*

*6 large red bell
peppers*

1/2 cup white vinegar

*1, 8 to 10-ounce can
crushed tomatoes*

*1 teaspoon garlic,
minced*

1 tablespoon sugar

2 teaspoons salt

*2 tablespoons chopped
cilantro or parsley*

*16 ounces fettuccine,
cooked*

Grilled Chicken with Roasted Red Pepper Sauce and Pasta

Mix the oil, tarragon vinegar, and spice mixture and marinate the chicken for 6 hours.

Roast the whole peppers on an ungreased baking sheet in a 400° oven, until the skins are slightly charred. Remove and immediately wrap in plastic. When cool enough to handle, unwrap and scrape away the skin and seeds. Purée the peppers, white vinegar, tomatoes, salt, garlic and sugar. Heat and simmer for 20 minutes. Season to taste (may need garlic, salt or sugar.) Thin with water if desired. Grill the chicken, then slice. Arrange the pasta on plates. Spoon on the sauce and layer chicken strips on top. Sprinkle with the cilantro. SERVES 4

*Courtesy of Bev & Lou Gerber,
Café Europa*

Grilled Grouper over Pineapple Salsa

Mix all of the ingredients other than the grouper and let marinate for 3 hours minimum (overnight if possible.)

Grill the grouper on one side, about 4 minutes. When flipped, add the salsa to the hot plate. Cook until the liquid has evaporated and serve over the fish.

SERVES 4

4, 6-ounce grouper fillets
1 medium pineapple, cored, peeled and diced
1/2 small yellow pepper, diced
1/2 small red pepper, diced
1 small red onion, diced
2 cloves garlic, minced
1 jalapeno, diced
1 lime, zest and juice
1 lemon, zest and juice
6 tablespoons white wine
1/4 cup raspberry vinegar

Chef Scott Sundermeyer,
Hyatt Regency

Grilled Tuna with Pineapple Chutney

6, 1" thick tuna steaks
1 pineapple, peeled
   and cored
1 red pepper
1 medium onion
3 tablespoons olive oil
1 tablespoon flour
pinch of allspice
pinch of cumin
1/4 cup honey
1/4 cup apple juice
pinch of cayenne
   pepper

To prepare the chutney, cut the pineapple, onion and red pepper into 1/4" pieces. Heat the oil in a medium pan on high. Add the onion and sauté until tender. Add the flour and stir. Stir in the red pepper, pineapple and allspice. Add the apple juice, cumin, cayenne and honey. Bring to a boil. Cover and reduce to low. Cook for 1 hour, stirring occasionally. Remove from the heat. May be served chilled or warm.

To prepare the tuna, brush the tuna steaks with olive oil and grill 4 minutes on each side. Remove to a platter, cover with chutney and serve.
SERVES 6

Chef Richard Canestrari,
Café at Wexford

Grouper Glacage

Glacage:

Bake the grouper in a 375° oven for 10-15 minutes, or until flaky. Dice the leeks, chives, bacon and mushrooms, and sauté in the butter for 2 - 3 minutes. Add the wine, bring to a boil and cook until the wine evaporates. Cool.

Blend together the cheese and sour cream. Add the cooled glacage mixture and salt and pepper to taste. Spoon 1/2 of the glasage mixture onto each piece of cooked fish. Return to the oven until brown.
SERVES 2

2, 8-ounce grouper fillets
1/2 cup leeks or onions
1/4 cup chives
5 slices cooked bacon
1/2 cup mushrooms
3 tablespoons butter
1/2 cup white wine
3/4 cup Boursin cheese
3/4 cup sour cream
salt and white pepper

Chef Cynthia Hair,
Hemingway's, Hyatt Regency

Lamb Chops à la Landon

*2, 8-ounce 3/4" thick
lamb chops
1/4 pound melted
butter
2 tablespoons sherry
mint jelly
2 cloves garlic, minced
1 teaspoon black
pepper
1 teaspoon seasoned
salt
pinch of thyme
1/2 stick margarine
1 teaspoon onion
powder*

Rub the chops until well coated with garlic, pepper, seasoned salt, thyme, margarine and onion powder. Melt the butter in a skillet. When hot, sear the chops until dark on one side. Turn, cover, and reduce the heat. Cook until desired doneness.

Deglaze* the pan with the sherry and serve the chops with pan juices and mint jelly. Serve with parsleyed red skin potatoes and asparagus with hollandaise.

SERVES 2

* See glossary.

*Chef Brad Terhune,
Fitzgerald's*

Lobster Gruyère

Bring the sherry, chicken stock, lemon juice, mustard and pepper to a boil. Add the Gruyère and half-and-half, whisking constantly. Thicken with the roux. Sauté the lobster and mushrooms. Place in an ovenproof casserole dish. Top with the sauce and sprinkle with Parmesan cheese. Place in a 350° oven or under a broiler until brown.
SERVES 4 - 6

12 ounces lobster meat
1 cup mushrooms, sliced
1/2 cup sherry
*2 cups chicken stock**
1 tablespoon lemon juice
2 tablespoons Dijon mustard
1/4 tablespoon white pepper
1 cup Gruyère cheese, grated
1/2 cup half-and-half
*1 1/2 tablespoons roux***
Parmesan cheese

** May subsitute with chicken broth.*

*** See glossary.*

Chef Jeff Hendrickson,
Sea Pines Plantation Club

Marinated Mahi Mahi

3 cups apple cider
6 tablespoons soy sauce
1/4 pound unsalted
 butter
1 tablespoon garlic,
 minced
4 Mahi fillets, 8-10
 ounces each

Bring the cider, soy sauce, butter and garlic to a boil. Reduce by half. Cool to room temperature. Marinate the Mahi fillets for at least 12 hours in the cider mixture. Grill over charcoal.
SERVES 4

*Chef Johnny Highberger,
High Z's*

Marinated Oven-Roasted Tenderloin

Place the tenderloin, onion, garlic and herbs in a large pan. Pour the wine and 1 cup of the oil over the meat and season. Marinate for 6 hours.

Sear the tenderloin in a large saucepan with 2 tablespoons of oil until browned all over. Roast for 15 - 18 minutes in a preheated 400° oven until medium rare. Remove to a warm plate and set aside.

To prepare the coulis, seed and coarsely chop each color pepper and place in separate pans. To each, add 1 chopped onion, 3 cups water, 3 tablespoons oil and season to taste. Boil until softened. Purée each separately in a food processor until smooth. Strain and season. Pour the coulis on the plate in red and yellow stripes. Slice the tenderloin and place around the sauce.
SERVES 8 - 10

Chef Jim McLain,
formerly of Wexford Plantation,
currently of Callawassie Island

Tenderloin:
2 to 3 pound center-cut tenderloin
1 large onion, chopped
1 large clove garlic, chopped,
2 sprigs rosemary, chopped
2 sprigs thyme, chopped
1 cup red wine
1 cup plus 2 tablespoons peanut oil
season to taste

*Coulis:**
6 red bell peppers
6 golden bell peppers
2 large onions
6 cups water
6 tablespoons oil
season to taste

** See glossary.*

Marinated Salmon in Basil and Olive Oil

1 1/2 pounds fresh
  Norwegian salmon
2 tablespoons extra -
  virgin olive oil
2 tablespoons lemon
  and lime juice
2 tablespoons chopped
  basil
1 tablespoon crushed
  pepper
1 tablespoon crushed
  coriander seeds
salt

Peel and skin the salmon. Refrigerate for 2 hours. Chill 4 plates.

Using a very sharp knife, thinly slice the salmon without breaking the meat. Brush the bottom of the plates with lemon/lime juice. Place the salmon on the plates and brush the fish very lightly with the juice. Season with the salt, pepper, coriander and basil. Then brush the salmon with olive oil. Chill for 2 hours. Serve with French white toast and a glass of Chardonnay.

SERVES 4

Chef Jean-Loup Kunckler,
The Gaslight

Marinated Swordfish with Cilantro Lime Butter

Let the butter come to room temperature. In a mixing bowl, whip butter until fluffy. Add 1/4 cup cilantro, pepper, salt and lime juice and mix. Place the butter mixture on a sheet of plastic wrap and roll into an even cylinder, using the wrap to shape. Chill.

Mix the soy sauce, oil, remaining cilantro, garlic, ginger, red pepper and honey. Marinate the steaks for 24 hours.

Grill the steaks over medium heat 4-5 minutes per side, or until it is firm to the touch. Top each steak with a 1/2" slice of cilantro-lime butter. SERVES 4

1/2 pound butter
3/4 cup fresh cilantro, chopped
1 tablespoon cracked black pepper
1 teaspoon salt
juice of 4 limes
4, 7-ounce swordfish or tuna steaks
2 cups soy sauce
1/4 cup olive oil
3 cloves garlic, minced
1/4 cup fresh ginger, minced
2 tablespoons red pepper, crushed
1/4 cup honey

*Chef Sonny Tanksley,
Long Cove Club*

Norwegian Salmon in Champagne Fennel Sauce

1, 7-ounce salmon fillet
Flour, seasoned with salt and pepper
1/4 cup oil
1/4 cup champagne
2 tablespoons vermouth
1 teaspoon shallots, chopped
1 teaspoon fennel, finely chopped
1 tablespoon lemon juice
2 tablespoons heavy cream
1 tablespoon butter
4 ounces linguini, cooked

Dredge the salmon in the seasoned flour and sauté in heated oil. Drain the oil into another pan for the sauce. Place the salmon in a 200° oven to keep warm. Start the sauce by adding the wine and vermouth to the oil. Add the shallots, fennel and juice. Add the cream and butter, stirring constantly. Return the salmon to the sauce and serve over linguini.

SERVES 1

Chef Robert Montbleau,
Port Royal Plantation Clubhouse

Oven Steamed Salmon and Scallop Terrine

Preheat the oven to 400°. Fillet the salmon, removing the skin and bones. Remove the muscles from the scallops. Put the scallops in a food processor and add the lemon juice, soy sauce, Tabasco, parsley, eggs, and process. Slowly add the cream until blended. Season with salt and pepper.

Thinly slice the salmon. Grease a terrine* with butter. Alternate layers of the salmon and the scallop mousse until full. Cover with waxed paper and bake for 25-30 minutes. Remove and set aside.

To prepare the sauce, cut the bell peppers into diamond shapes. Combine with the wine and the dill in a sauté pan and reduce by half. Add the butter, and reduce until creamy. Season with salt and pepper.

Serve slices of the terrine with the warm sauce on top.
SERVES 6-8
*See glossary.

Chef Jim McLain,
formerly of Wexford Plantation,
currently of Callawassie Island

2 pounds fresh
  Norwegian salmon
1 1/2 pounds fresh sea
  scallops
juice of 1 lemon
2 tablespoons soy sauce
1/2 teaspoon Tabasco
  pepper sauce
4 tablespoons parsley,
  chopped
6 eggs
1/2 cup heavy cream

Sauce:
2 tablespoons fresh
  dill, chopped
3 roasted gold bell
  peppers, peeled and
  seeded**
3 cups white wine
1 cup herb butter,
  softened
salt and pepper to
  taste

** May use yellow
peppers.

Oysters Gourmet

*64 oysters, cleaned
and on half-shell
1, 8-ounce can of
clams with juice,
chopped
2 quarts heavy cream
2 tablespoons chives
pinch of saffron
salt and pepper
1 pound crabmeat
fresh bread crumbs
Parmesan cheese,
grated
rock salt*

*Butter Roux:
1 pound butter
1 pound flour*

To prepare the roux, combine the butter and flour. Cook over moderate heat for 10 minutes. Do not brown or burn.

Place the chopped clams and juice in a saucepan and bring to a soft boil. Add the cream, chives, saffron, salt and pepper. Thicken the mixture with the butter roux. Cook gently for 8-11 minutes, stirring occasionally. Let cool. Mixture should be thick enough to spread on top of the oysters.

Clean the crabmeat of any shells. Place a generous amount of crabmeat on top of each oyster. Place some of the clam sauce mixture over the crabmeat, covering the oysters. Top with the fresh bread crumbs and Parmesan cheese. Bake on a bed of rock salt in a 350° oven for approximately 12-15 minutes.
SERVES 8

*Chef Michael Zornouski,
The Westin Resort*

Pasta and Shrimp

Melt the margarine in a large skillet and sauté the shrimp with the garlic and mushrooms until the shrimp turn pink, about 2 minutes. Add the cream, onions, and tomatoes, seasoning with salt and pepper to taste. The cream will erupt and begin to reduce. Add the cooked pasta and toss. The pasta will help absorb the cream as it thickens. When the cream begins to get sticky, remove from the heat. Sprinkle the dish with the Parmesan cheese and chopped parsley.

For variety, add steamed or blanched vegetables as the cream thickens.
SERVES 4

6 cups cooked pasta (tortellini or fettuccine)
2 tablespoons margarine
1 pound medium-sized shrimp, peeled and deveined
1 1/2 teaspoons garlic, minced
1 cup mushrooms, sliced
1/2 pint heavy cream
6 green onions, chopped
3 tablespoons sun-dried tomatoes, chopped
salt and white pepper
Parmesan cheese to taste
parsley, chopped

Chef Scott Miller,
Charlie's

2 tablespoons butter
2 tablespoons olive oil
1 tablespoon shallots
2 tablespoons pro-
    sciutto ham, finely
    diced
1 teaspoon garlic,
    chopped
1/4 cup zucchini,
    halved and sliced
1/4 cup heavy cream
pinch of basil
pinch of parsley
2 tablespoons
    Parmesan cheese,
    grated
2 tablespoons Romano
    cheese, grated
salt and pepper

Pasta with Zucchini and Prosciutto

Sauté the shallots and prosciutto in the oil and butter. Add the garlic and zucchini. Add the cream, basil, parsley and cheeses to thicken. Season with the salt and pepper and serve over fettuccine.
SERVES 1

Chef Robert Montbleau,
Port Royal Plantation Clubhouse

ENTREES

Pheasant Monticello

Sauté the vegetables and apples. Add the wine and reduce by 3/4. Add the seasoning, spice, bread crumbs and cream. Cook until sticky, then cool. Stuff the pheasant with the crumb mixture. Wrap the pheasant in the grape leaves. Wrap the bacon around the grape leaves and skewer. Bake in a 325° oven until golden brown.
SERVES 1

1 1/2 teaspoons diced celery
1 1/2 teaspoons diced onions
1 1/2 teaspoons diced apples
1/4 cup white wine
pinch of fresh tarragon, finely chopped
pinch of chervil, finely chopped
salt and pepper to taste
1 ounce white bread crumbs, cut into 1/4" squares
1/4 cup cream
1 baby pheasant, boned completely from back, leaving leg joints
2 grape leaves
1 piece bacon

Chef Gerard Thompson,
Windows on Harbour Town

Plantation Club Scampi

10 large shrimp,
  peeled and deveined
1 tablespoon fresh
  minced garlic
2 tablespoons clarified
  butter*
1/4 cup sherry
1/4 cup chicken
  stock, or broth
1 tablespoon chopped
  parsley
1/2 cup bread crumbs,
  finely chopped
1 tablespoon lemon
  juice

* See glossary.

Sauté the shrimp and garlic in the butter. When the shrimp is almost cooked, remove from the pan and add the sherry, chicken stock and lemon juice. Bring to a boil and reduce heat. Blend in the bread crumbs. Add the parsley and shrimp. Simmer until the sauce thickens slightly. Serve with thinly sliced French bread and lemon wedges.
SERVES 2

Chef Jeff Hendrickson,
Sea Pines Plantation Club

Quail with Mustard Sauce

Dredge the quail in flour and sauté in butter. Brown both sides and remove from the pan.

Deglaze the pan with the brandy and add the remaining ingredients. Add the quail and cover. Simmer for 10-15 minutes.

SERVES 4

8 semi-boneless quail
1 cup all-purpose flour
1/4 cup butter
1/3 cup brandy
3/4 cup chicken stock, or chicken broth
1 tablespoon Dijon mustard
1/2 teaspoon lemon juice
1 teaspoon Worcestershire sauce
1/4 teaspoon pepper

Chef Jeff Hendrickson,
Sea Pines Plantation Club

Rabbit Sautéed with Dijon Mustard

1, 3-pound rabbit, in 6 pieces*
salt and pepper
1/2 cup Dijon mustard
5 tablespoons butter
1/4 pound salt pork
1/2 pound pearl onions
3 cloves garlic, peeled
bouquet garni of thyme, bayleaf, and parsley**
1 cup white wine
6 large mushrooms, quartered
1 tablespoon lemon juice
1/4 cup heavy cream

*Roasting chicken or capon may be substituted.

**See glossary.

Rinse the rabbit meat under water, then salt and pepper and coat with mustard. Heat the butter in a high-sided frying pan until it foams, adding the rabbit, pork, onions, garlic and bouquet garni. Cook on medium-high heat for 20 minutes, turning often. Add the wine, scraping often to keep from sticking. Add the mushrooms. Cook over moderate heat for 15 minutes. Lower the heat, cover and simmer for 10 minutes. Remove the meat and onions to a hot platter. Whisk in the heavy cream. If all the wine has evaporated, add a 1/2 cup of water. Heat almost to boiling. Whisk in the lemon juice. Correct spices to taste. Spoon over the rabbit.
SERVES 4

*Chef Dave Plemmons,
Renaissance*

Red Snapper Casino

To prepare the Casino butter, soften the butter and mix with all of the ingredients. Roll into a 1 1/2" diameter log and wrap in plastic. Refrigerate until needed.

To prepare the red snapper dredge the snapper in the flour. Heat a sauté pan and sauté the snapper, skin side up. In a separate pan, melt the Casino butter. Add the remaining ingredients, except the julienned vegetables.

Cover the bottom of a plate with the julienned vegetables and top them with the fish, clams and Casino Butter.
SERVES 1

Chef Michael Sigler,
The Westin Resort

7 ounces red snapper fillet
2 tablespoons flour
1/4 cup butter
4 small clams
1 tablespoon chopped raw bacon
1 tablespoon parsley, chopped
1 tablespoon white wine
1/2 lemon
2 tablespoons julienne of mixed vegetables, such as carrots, zucchini, yellow squash, etc.

Casino Butter:
1 pound unsalted butter
1/4 cup shallots, diced
1 cup green peppers, diced
1 cup red peppers, diced
1 tablespoon Tabasco pepper sauce
1/2 cup white wine.

Red Snapper in Pecan Crust with Valencia Butter

4, 8-ounce red snapper fillets
1/2 cup flour
2 eggs, beaten
1 pound ground pecans
1 cup butter
1/4 cup heavy cream
1/4 cup sour cream
1/2 cup undiluted orange juice concentrate
1 cup whole sweet butter, chilled and cubed

Dip the fish in flour, then into the beaten eggs. Pat the fish with the ground pecans, pressing firmly. In a medium pan over medium heat, melt the butter and add the fish. Sauté on each side, about 3-4 minutes. (Take care not to brown the nuts too much.) Remove the fish and place in a 350° oven in a covered dish for 10-15 minutes or until done. Combine the heavy cream and sour cream with the orange juice. Boil for 2 minutes. Remove from the heat and whisk in the cold, cubed butter, one cube at a time. Serve the fish on top of the sauce.

SERVES 4

Chef Scott Sundermeyer,
Hyatt Regency

Salmon Med

Coat the salmon in flour and pan fry in a small amount of butter. Remove from the pan. Sauté the artichokes, tomatoes and olives. Add the wine and cook for 2-3 minutes. Add the crumbled feta cheese. Remove from the heat and serve on top of the salmon.
SERVES 1

1 salmon fillet
1/2 cup flour
2 teaspoons butter
3 artichoke hearts
1/4 cup diced tomatoes
2 tablespoon black olives, sliced
1/4 cup white wine
3 teaspoons feta cheese

Chef Cynthia Hair,
Hemingway's, Hyatt Regency

2 tablespoons shallots,
  minced
1/4 cup white wine
1/4 cup cream
2 tablespoons lump
  crabmeat
3 leaves of phyllo
  dough
2 tablespoons butter
1, 6-ounce salmon
  fillet
1 tablespoon spinach
  leaves, blanched
salt and pepper

Salmon in Phyllo Dough

Sauté half of the shallots and add half of the wine. Add half of the cream and reduce the heat, stirring until thick. Add the crabmeat and cool.

Lay the phyllo leaves on a dry table. Brush butter between the layers. Lay the salmon 3/4 of the way down on the phyllo leaves and put the crab mixture and spinach on top. Fold the top of the leaves over the stuffing and roll the edges like a papillote.* Butter the outside liberally and completely.

Sauté the remaining shallots and wine. Reduce the heat and add the cream. Reduce to desired thickness. Bake the pockets in a 300° oven until brown. Top with the sauce.
SERVES 1

* See glossary.

Chef Gerard Thompson,
Windows on Harbour Town

Scalloped Pork Chops with Oyster Dressing

To prepare the dressing, melt the butter and add the onion, red pepper and celery. Cook for 1 minute on medium-high heat. Add the water and oysters with liquid and heat to a boil. Add the crackers. Season with salt, pepper and Worcestershire sauce.

Sprinkle the pork chops liberally with the pepper, salt, garlic and onion powder on both sides. Place them in a baking dish and cover them with the oyster dressing. Fill the dish with the hot milk just to the top of the oyster dressing and bake, covered, for 1 hour, 15 minutes in a 350° oven.
SERVES 4

1 stick butter
1 cup onion, diced
1 cup red bell peppers, diced
1 cup celery, diced
1 cup water
1/2 pint oysters with liquid
3 1/2 cups crackers, crushed
Worcestershire sauce
4, 1/2" thick pork chops
salt and pepper
1 clove garlic, minced
onion powder
2 tablespoons butter
2 cups hot milk

Chef Brad Terhune,
Fitzgerald's

1 tablespoon butter
1/2 cup diced carrots
1/2 cup diced celery
*1/2 teaspoon crab base**
1/2 teaspoon lobster
 *base**
1/2 teaspoon shrimp
 *base**
1 quart whipping
 cream
2 cups milk
1/4 cup sherry
1/8 teaspoon cumin,
 ground
1/8 teaspoon dill
3 cups cooked seafood
6 crêpe shells

** See glossary.*

Seafood Crêpes

Sauté the carrots and celery in the butter. Add the remaining ingredients and whisk over low heat until bubbly and thickened. Put your favorite cooked seafood in crêpes and follow directions for the chicken crepes on page 65.
SERVES 6

Chef Deborah Van Plew,
Flamingo's Café

Seafood Quiche

Heat a medium sauté pan and add the butter. Brown all of the seafood and season with half of the salt and pepper. Set aside.

In a separate bowl, whip the eggs lightly, then add the cream. Whip in the remaining salt, pepper and thyme. Fold the browned seafood and cheese into the egg mixture. Put half into each shell and bake 325° for 45 minutes. Remove from the oven and let stand 15 minutes before serving.

YIELD: 8 large slices

1/2 cup butter
10 medium to large shrimp
1/2 pound scallops
6 ounces crabmeat
1/4 teaspoon salt
1/8 teaspoon pepper
8 eggs
1 quart heavy cream
1 teaspoon thyme
2 cups grated Swiss cheese
2, 9" pie shells, unbaked

Chef Robert A. Fedorko,
The Westin Resort

1/2 onion, diced
1 tablespoon butter
1 1/4 cups rice
2 cups chicken stock,
   or chicken broth
salt and pepper
3 pounds large
   shrimp, cleaned and
   deveined
1 onion, sliced
1 red pepper, sliced
1 green pepper, sliced
pinch of basil
1 pint cherry tomatoes
2 - 4 tablespoons
   Pernod

**See glossary.

Shrimp Pernod over Rice

Sauté the diced onion in the butter and add the rice, chicken stock, salt and pepper. Simmer for 5 minutes. Cover and bake for 30 minutes in a 350° oven. Sauté the shrimp with the sliced onion and peppers until the vegetables start to soften. Add the basil, salt and pepper. Allow to cook for 3 minutes. Add the tomatoes and Pernod to taste. Allow Pernod to flame. Serve over rice.
SERVES 6

*Chef Mark Christian,
William F. Pelican Restaurant*

Smoked Caribbean Meat Pie

Heat the oil and add the onions, peppers, garlic, thyme, and parsley. Add the pork, olives, red peppers, tomatoes, and simmer until the liquid reduces and the mixture coats a spoon. Mix the sherry, vinegar and mustard until dissolved. Add to the meat and vegetables and mix well. Remove from the pan.

Combine the flour, salt and shortening. Rub the mixture together until it resembles coarse meal Pour ice water over the mixture and toss until the dough holds together. Roll the dough into a cylinder about 12" long and 2" in diameter. Cut into 2" segments, then roll each segment into a 6" circle. Put 1/3 cup of the warm filling mixture in the center of the circle and egg wash the edges. Fold the dough in half until the edges meet. With a floured fork, press the edges down to seal. Brush the surface of the pie with the melted butter and bake on a buttered sheet pan at 350° for 20 minutes or until the crust is golden.
SERVES 6

Chef Sonny Tanksley,
Long Cove Club

3 tablespoons olive oil
Finely chop:
  1 cup onion
  1/2 cup green pepper
  1 tablespoon garlic
  1 tablespoon fresh
    thyme
  1 tablespoon parsley
  2 tablespoons green
    and black olives
1 teaspoon red pepper,
  crushed
1, 2-pound smoked
pork shoulder,
  minced
2 cups tomatoes, diced
2 tablespoons sherry
1 tablespoon balsamic
  vinegar
3/4 teaspoon dry
  mustard
2 1/2 cups flour
1/2 teaspoon salt
3/4 cup shortening
4-6 tablespoons ice
  water
1 egg, beaten
1/4 cup butter, melted

2, 6-8 ounce chicken
breasts
1 sweet apple, peeled,
baked and diced
4 tablespoons butter
1/2 teaspoon cinnamon
1/4 cup sugar

Smoked Chicken Breast with Apple Butter

To prepare the apple butter, soften the butter to room temperature. Add the diced apple, cinnamon and sugar. Mix well.

To prepare the chicken, brush the chicken breasts with the apple butter. Smoke over hickory chips for two minutes on each side. Remove from the smoker and baste once again with the apple butter. Place the chicken in a 350° oven for 12-14 minutes or until done. Serve on a bed of lettuce or on a sandwich roll.

SERVES 2

*Chef Robert A. Fedorko,
The Westin Resort*

Snapper Fillets with Orange, Tomato and Cilantro Sauce

Salt and pepper the fish. In a medium saucepan, simmer the orange juice, tomato, garlic, shallots, cilantro, white wine, salt and pepper. Reduce the heat and whisk in the butter 1 tablespoon at a time, allowing each to melt before adding the next one. Bake, poach, broil or charbroil the fish. Coat with the sauce.

SERVES 6

2 1/2 to 3 pounds snapper fillets
salt and pepper
2/3 cup orange juice
1 tomato, peeled, seeded, diced
1/2 teaspoon garlic, minced
2 tablespoons shallots, minced
1 tablespoon fresh cilantro
1/4 cup white wine
1 stick unsalted butter

Chef Dean A. Thomas,
The Westin Resort

3 medium shallots, peeled
1 medium onion
2 pieces anchovy fillets
2 pounds boneless ribeye
salt and pepper
3 1/2 tablespoons butter
1/2 cup red wine

Steak, Wine-Growers Style

Chop the shallots, onion and anchovy fillets into very small pieces, or purée in a blender. Set aside.

Salt and pepper the steak. Heat the butter in a frying pan until it foams. Add the steak and cook over moderate heat for 6 minutes each side for rare or 8 minutes each side for medium.

Remove the steak and set on a warm platter. Add the onion, shallots and anchovy mixture to the pan drippings. Cook until the onions are soft and begin to brown. Add the wine. Cook at a boil for 1-2 minutes until the sauce thickens to coat a spoon. Strain.

Serve the sauce over steak or in a gravy boat.
SERVES 4

Chef Dave Plemmons,
Renaissance

Stuffed Chicken Legs with Mushrooms and Ham

Bone the chicken. Slice the basil leaves into very thin strips. In a saucepan, melt the butter. Add shallots, basil, garlic, mushrooms and ham. Cook for 10 minutes without browning, then add the cream and cook 10 minutes on medium heat. Add the salt and pepper. Stuff the chicken legs with the mixture and insert skewers. Using string to hold everything together, roast in a 450° oven for 15 minutes. Remove the string and skewers and slice the chicken.

SERVES 8

8 cooked chicken legs
3 basil leaves
1 teaspoon butter
2 large shallots, diced
2 garlic cloves, diced
1/2 pound mushrooms, diced
6 tablespoons ham, diced
1 cup whipping cream
salt and pepper
8 wooden skewers

Chef Jean-Loup Kunckler,
The Gaslight

1, 12-ounce package
    jumbo pasta shells
2, 9-ounce frozen
    creamed spinach (in
    cook-in-pouch)
15-ounce package
    Ricotta cheese
1 cup Mozzarella
    cheese, shredded
1 teaspoon salt
1/4 teaspoon pepper
1/2 pound ground
    beef*
1 quart marinara
    sauce**

*May substitute with
shrimp and scallops.

**May substitute
 with a cream seafood
sauce.

Stuffed Shells

Cook the shells as directed and drain. Prepare the spinach as directed on the pouch.

Open the spinach into a large bowl and cool slightly. Stir in the cheeses, salt and pepper. Stuff each shell with 1 tablespoon of mixture and place in an oven-proof pan. Cook the beef over medium heat until browned. Stir in the marinara sauce. Spoon the sauce over the shells. Cover with foil and bake at 350° for 30 minutes.

Note: this recipe will freeze well up to 3 months. Remove from freezer and bake for 50 minutes.

SERVES 10

*Chef Deborah Van Plew,
Flamingo's Café*

Tournedos au Poivre

Melt half of the butter in a large frying pan over medium-high heat. Add the steaks and sauté on both sides until medium rare. Remove from the pan. Set aside. Add the brandy, peppercorns, and shallots. Stir and ignite. When the flame dies down, add the brown gravy and red wine. Cook until sauce is reduced by 1/3. Stir in the remaining butter and parsley. Pour over steaks and serve.
SERVES 4

8, 3-ounce tenderloin steaks
1 cup butter
1/2 cup brandy
2 teaspoons green peppercorns
2 teaspoons minced shallots
1 cup brown gravy
1/2 cup red wine
2 teaspoons parsley, chopped

Courtesy of Bev & Lou Gerber,
Café Europa

1 cup shelled pecans
3 tablespoons fresh
oregano
1/2 cup bourbon
3 tablespoons lemon
vinegar
1/2 red bell pepper,
chopped
1/2 yellow bell pepper,
chopped
1 tablespoon sugar
4, 6-ounce fillets of
triggerfish
fresh cracked pepper
4 tablespoons butter
1/4 cup white wine
salt

Triggerfish with Sweet Pepper Pecan Confit

Thoroughly mix the pecans, oregano, bourbon and vinegar. Pour over the fish and marinate for 48 hours.

Remove the fish and add the bell peppers and sugar to the pecan mixture and bake in a 350° oven until the liquid evaporates. Brush the fish with the butter and wine. Top with the pecan mixture. Salt and pepper to taste. Broil until brown.
SERVES 4

Chef Dean A. Thomas,
The Westin Resort

Vealemince Calvados

Sauté the veal in the hot oil. Remove from the pan. Add the butter, shallots and mushrooms and sauté until shallots are clear. Add the wine and reduce by half. Add the brandy. Flame, and reduce. Add the cream and reduce consistency. Return the veal to the pan. Cook until hot. Serve over the blanched pasta. Top with the chives.
SERVES 1

Chef Gerard A. Thompson,
Windows on Harbour Town

5 ounces veal, cut into slim julienne strips*

1 1/2 teaspoons olive oil

1 tablespoon butter

1 1/2 teaspoons shallots, finely chopped

2 tablespoons chanterelle mushrooms, cut into slim julienne strips*

2 tablespoons white wine

1 tablespoon brandy

6 tablespoons cream

1 cup tri-color angel hair pasta, blanched al dente

1 1/2 teaspoons chives, cut into 1/2" strips

* See glossary.

3 tablespoons butter
1 cup sliced almonds
1 teaspoon garlic,
   chopped
1/4 cup prosciutto
1/4 cup brandy
1/2 cup demi-glace*
1/4 cup heavy cream
pinch of salt
pinch of pepper
1/4 cup oil
4, 1" thick veal chops

* See glossary.

Veal Chops with Golden Almonds, Prosciutto, and Brandy Cream

To prepare the sauce, in a small pan melt the butter over medium heat. Add the almonds and garlic, careful not to burn the garlic and cook until brown. Add the prosciutto and cook for 3 minutes. Add the brandy, flame, then add demi-glace and cream. Simmer for 10 minutes. Salt and pepper to taste.

To prepare the veal, preheat the oven to 350°. Heat the oil in a pan and sear the chops on both sides. Place the chops in the oven and cook for 10 minutes. Place on a platter with the sauce and serve.

SERVES 4

*Chef Richard Canestrari,
Café at Wexford*

Veal Colette

Cut the chard leaves into 1/4" pieces, blanch, then immerse them in ice water and strain. Peel the potatoes and place in water. Sauté the shallots in the butter until very hot. Dredge the veal in flour and place in the pan with the shallots. Add the potatoes. Sauté until golden brown and place on a plate. Deglaze the pan with the white wine and pour over the veal.
SERVES 4

1 head red Swiss chard*
8 small red potatoes
1 shallot, finely
   chopped
1 tablespoon butter
24 ounces veal
1/2 cup flour
1/4 cup white wine

* See glossary.

Chef Alain Tiphaine,
Capt's Table

1 lemon
1 cup flour, seasoned
with salt and pepper
2 eggs
1/4 cup salad oil
1 1/2 cups fresh bread
crumbs
4, 4-ounce veal cutlets

Viennese Wiener Schnitzel

Squeeze the juice from the lemon and set aside.

Put the flour mixture in a separate bowl and set aside.

Beat the eggs with 2 teaspoons salad oil in a separate bowl and set aside.

Chop, grind or crush the bread crumbs in a separate bowl. Set aside.

Pound out the veal with a mallet or the side of a heavy knife. Coat the veal with lemon and blot with a paper towel. Dredge the veal in seasoned flour, shaking off excess. Immerse the veal in the egg-oil mixture. Coat it with the bread crumbs and press the crumbs into the meat. Heat the remaining oil until very hot. Add the meat and reduce the heat to medium. Brown on both sides.
SERVES 4

Chef Dave Plemmons,
Renaissance

DESSERTS

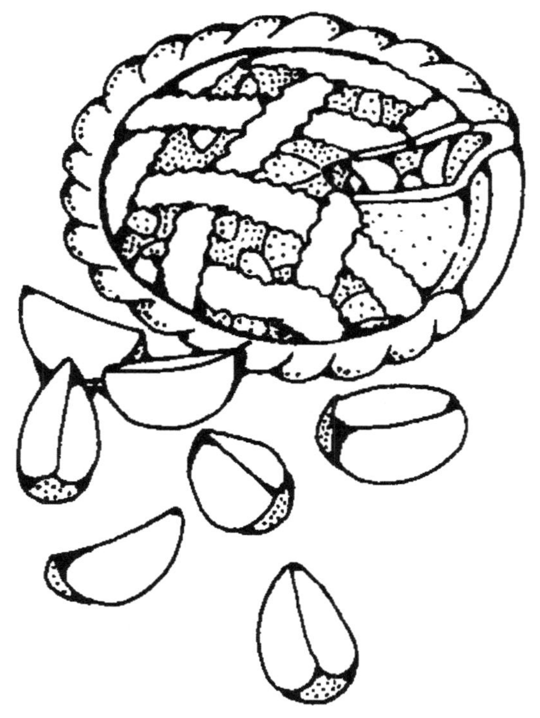

Almond Tuiles with Fresh Raspberries

Preheat the oven to 350°. Mix the sugar, flour, egg whites and salt. Beat to a thick batter. Add the almonds. Allow to sit 30 minutes.

Spray a cookie sheet with a non-stick spray, then pour about 4 1/2 teaspoons of batter per tuille. Bake 8-10 minutes until golden brown. Quickly place the hot tuiles over inverted cups to form baskets. Once cool, fill the baskets with the raspberries.

To prepare the crème anglaise, scald the milk with the vanilla extract. Combine the sugar, cornstarch and egg yolks. Whisk until pale and creamy. Slowly add the milk. Place the mixture in a double boiler over hot water and whisk for 10 minutes until the sauce coats the back of a wooden spoon. Remove the bowl from the double boiler and rest it in ice water.

To serve, place a little sauce on each plate and place the tuile on the sauce. Garnish with a few raspberries and fresh sprigs of mint.
SERVES 4-6

Chef Jim McLain,
formerly of Wexford Plantation,
currently of Callawassie Island

Tuiles:
3/4 cup powdered
 sugar, sifted
3/4 cup all-purpose
 flour
3 large egg whites
pinch of salt
2 tablespoons slivered
 almonds

Filling:
2 cups fresh raspberries
1/4 cup powdered
 sugar, sifted

Crème anglaise:
1 1/2 cups milk
2 teaspoons vanilla
 extract
1/2 cup sugar
1 teaspoon cornstarch
4 large egg yolks

Garnish:
1/2 cup fresh raspberries
2 stems fresh mint

2 cups shortening

4 cups sugar

6 eggs, beaten

4 cups bananas, mashed

3 cups nuts, chopped

6 cups flour

4 teaspoons baking soda

2 teaspoons salt

1 tablespoon cinnamon

1 cup raisins

1 cup coconut, toasted

Banana Nut Muffins

Cream the shortening and add the sugar and eggs. Mix well. Add the bananas and nuts. Mix well.

In a separate bowl, mix together the flour, soda and salt. Combine with banana mixture and beat 2 minutes. Stir in the cinnamon, raisins and coconut.

Pour into greased muffin tins and bake at 350° for 40-45 minutes.

YIELDS 30 - 40 muffins

Chef Robert Montbleau,
Port Royal Plantation Clubhouse

Bavarian Apple Tart

Cream together the butter, sugar, egg and vanilla. Gradually add the sifted flour to the creamed mixture. Form the dough into a ball, flatten it between sheets of wax paper and refrigerate for 1 hour.

Preheat oven to 350°. Roll the dough on a floured surface to 1/8" thick. Line a 12", 1 1/2" deep tart pan with the dough. Trim the edges.

Thoroughly mix the custard ingredients and set aside.

Slice the apples thinly and fan them out on the shell. Pour the filling over the apples and bake for 30 minutes until the custard sets. Cool and brush with the melted apricot jam.

SERVES 6-8

Dough:
1 pound butter,
  softened
2 cups sugar
1 egg
1/2 teaspoon vanilla
  extract
2 cups flour, sifted

Custard:
1/2 cup sugar
1/2 cup sour cream
1/2 cup heavy cream
2 eggs
1/2 teaspoon cinnamon

Filling:
6 medium apples,
  cored and peeled
apricot jam, melted

Courtesy Bev & Lou Gerber,
Café Europa

Chocolate Chip Pie

2 medium eggs
1/2 cup sugar
1/2 cup brown sugar
1/4 cup flour
1 cup melted butter,
  cooled
3/4 cup semi-sweet
  chocolate chips
1/2 cup walnuts,
  chopped
1, 9" pie shell,
  un-cooked

Beat the eggs in a bowl, adding the sugar, brown sugar and flour. Continuing to mix, add the butter, then the chocolate chips and walnuts. Mix well. Pour into the pie shell and bake at 325° until browned.

Note: Bake the pie immediately. Do not let it stand after it is mixed.

SERVES 8

Chef Anthony Mastropole,
Hyatt Regency

Chocolate Mousse Pie

To prepare the crust, combine the crumbs and the butter. Press onto the bottom and sides of a 10" springform pan. Chill for 30 minutes.

To prepare the filling, soften the chocolate in a double boiler or microwave. Scrape into a bowl and add the whole eggs. Mix well, keeping the mixture warm. Add the egg yolks and mix until blended.

Whip the cream with powdered sugar until soft peaks form. Set aside.

Beat the egg whites until stiff but not dry. Stir a little of the cream mixture and a little of the egg whites into the chocolate mixture to lighten. Fold in the remaining cream and the remaining egg whites until completely blended. Pour into the crust and chill for 6 hours. After the pie has set, whip the remaining cups of heavy cream, powdered sugar and vanilla. Loosen the crust of the pie on all sides, using a sharp knife. Remove from the springform pan. Spread all but 1/2 of the cup of whipped cream over the top of the mousse. Pipe the remaining cream in the shells on top of the pie. Sprinkle the top with shaved chocolate and serve.

SERVES 14

Chef Anthony Mastropole,
Hyatt Regency

Crust:
3 cups Oreo cookie crumbs
1/2 cup unsalted butter, melted

Filling:
2 cups semi-sweet chocolate
2 medium eggs
4 medium egg yolks
2 cups heavy cream
6 tablespoons powdered sugar
4 medium egg whites

Topping:
2 cups heavy cream
1/4 cup powdered sugar
1 teaspoon vanilla
semi-sweet chocolate, shaved

5 1/2 ounces semi-
    sweet chocolate
3 tablespoons water
4 egg yolks
10 tablespoons
    granulated sugar
2 tablespoons Tia
    Maria
1/2 teaspoon
    cinnamon, ground
6 egg whites
1 pinch salt
1 tablespoon butter,
    melted
powdered sugar

Chocolate Tia Maria Soufflé

Preheat the oven to 425°. Melt the chocolate with the water in a microwave on medium for 3-4 minutes.

In a bowl, beat the egg yolks and 6 tablespoons of sugar until pale and creamy. Stir in the chocolate. Add the Tia Maria and the cinnamon and set aside.

In a bowl, beat the egg whites and the salt until stiff peaks form. Fold half of the egg whites into the chocolate mixture until the color is uniform. Lightly fold in the rest of the egg whites. Uniformity of color is not necessary at this stage.

Butter 4 small soufflé dishes, coating the inside with the remaining 4 tablespoons of sugar. Pour the batter into each and smooth. Bake for 10-20 minutes until the soufflés are twice their original height. Remove from the oven and sprinkle with the powdered sugar, serving immediately.
SERVES 4

*Chef Jim McLain,
formerly of Wexford Plantation,
currently of Callawassie Island*

Cold Chocolate Sauce

Chop the chocolate. Boil the water and sugar to make a simple syrup. Cool for 5 minutes. Place the chopped chocolate in a bowl and pour the syrup over it. Whip until the chocolate is completely melted. Let mixture set overnight at room temperature. Whip it before serving to make it smooth again.

1 3/4 cups semi-sweet chocolate
2 cups water
1 1/4 cup sugar

Chef Thierry Saglier,
Harbour Lights Bakery

Double Chocolate Torte with White Chocolate Sauce

Pastry:
1 1/4 cups all-purpose flour
3/4 stick unsalted butter
2 tablespoons vegetable shortening
1/4 teaspoon salt
3 tablespoons ice water

Chocolate Filling:
1 cup semi-sweet chocolate
1/2 cup unsalted butter
4 eggs
1/4 teaspoon salt
2 cups sugar
1 1/2 teaspoons vanilla
1 cup all-purpose flour, sifted

White Chocolate Sauce:
1 1/2 cups white chocolate
3 cups powdered sugar, sifted
3/4 cup heavy cream
3 tablespoons unsalted butter, softened
2 pinches of salt

Blend the first four pastry ingredients until it resembles coarse meal. Add the water and toss until the water is absorbed. Form a ball and knead lightly to distribute the fat. Dust with flour and chill for 30 minutes. Grease a tart pan with a non-stick spray. Roll the dough on a floured surface until wider than the pan. Line the pan with dough and pre-bake for 15 minutes.

Blend the chocolate and the butter until smooth. Combine the eggs and the salt. Whisk until foamy. Gradually add the sugar and vanilla and whip until a ribbon forms when you remove the whisk. Add the chocolate mixture and the flour. Blend well. Pour into the shell and bake at 375° for 25-30 minutes.

To prepare the sauce, melt the white chocolate in a double boiler for about 8 - 10 minutes. Transfer it to a bowl and cool slightly. Add the sugar and whisk until smooth. Mix in the cream, butter and salt. To serve, slice the torte and cover with the white chocolate sauce.
SERVES 6-8

Chef Jim McLain
formerly of Wexford Plantation,
currently of Callawassie Island

Frozen Raspberry Soufflé

Make a collar of waxed paper around a soufflé dish, extending it above the rim. Dissolve the gelatin in a small amount of hot water. Beat the egg yolks and 1/2 cup of the sugar until light yellow in color. Add the gelatin and warm it in a double boiler until it thickens and coats a spoon. Add the raspberry purée and the Chambord. Transfer to a larger bowl. Refrigerate for 30 minutes.

Beat the egg whites and gradually add 7 tablespoons of sugar until stiff. Fold into the raspberry mixture. Whip the cream with the remaining sugar until soft peaks form. Fold into the raspberry mixture. Pour into the soufflé dish. Freeze for 4 hours before serving.
SERVES 6-8

2 packages unflavored gelatin
8 egg yolks
1 1/4 cups sugar
1 cup raspberry purée
4 tablespoons Chambord
4 egg whites
1 1/2 cups heavy cream

Chef Thierry Saglier,
Harbour Lights Bakery

Grand Marnier Soufflé

Soufflé:
1 cup milk
5 egg yolks
1/4 cup flour
1/4 cup sugar
2 tablespoons brandy
1/4 cup Grand
   Marnier
8 egg whites

Topping:
1/4 cup cream
1/4 cup sugar
1 tablespoon brandy
2 tablespoons Grand
   Marnier

Combine the milk, egg yolks, flour and sugar. Cook over a double boiler, whisking constantly until thick and smooth. Add the brandy and Grand Marnier.

Beat the egg whites until stiff. Fold into the mixture. Butter and sprinkle sugar inside a small soufflé dish. Fill and bake at 350° for 35-40 minutes.

Serve with freshly whipped cream flavored with the sugar, brandy and Grand Marnier.
SERVES 4-6

Chef Jeff Hendrickson,
Sea Pines Plantation Club

Hot Rothschild Soufflé

Butter and sugar a soufflé dish. Boil the milk with the butter and sugar. Remove from the heat. Add the flour slowly and mix well. Add the egg yolks one at a time. Let the mixture cool. Add the Grand Marnier. Whip the egg whites until stiff. Fold into the mixture and add the raisins. Pour into the soufflé dish. Bake at 450° for 30 minutes. Top with the English Cream Sauce and serve.

To prepare the English cream sauce, beat the sugar and yolks until light yellow. Boil the milk and pour over the egg yolk mixture and stir. Pour the mixture back into the saucepan and stir over low heat until the sauce coats the spoon. Strain and add your favorite flavoring.

SERVES 6

Soufflé:
2 cups milk
6 tablespoons butter
3/4 cup sugar
7 ounces flour
10 eggs, separated
Grand Marnier to taste
raisins

English Cream Sauce:
3/4 cup sugar
5 egg yolks
12 cups milk
*vanilla extract**

**May substitute Amaretto or Grand Marnier.*

Chef Thierry Saglier,
Harbor Lights Bakery

Lintzertorte

2 cups flour
1 cup unsalted butter
1 cup sugar
1 egg
1 egg yolk
1 1/4 pounds almonds,
   finely ground and
   toasted
1/2 teaspoon
   cinnamon
zest of 2 lemons
1/2 cup raspberry jam

Combine all of the ingredients except the jam. Form into a firm ball and refrigerate for 1-2 hours or overnight. Reserve 1/4 of the dough for a lattice top. Roll the remaining dough into a 10" circle, placing into a pie pan. Spread the circle with the jam. Form a lattice top. Bake in a 375° degree oven until the jam bubbles and the top is light brown. Serve with whipped cream and fresh raspberries.
SERVES 10-12

Chef Chad Newman,
Charlie's

Peanut Butter Pie with Fudge Topping

To prepare the crust, butter a 9" pie pan. Mix all of the ingredients. Press into the pan and chill for 30 minutes.

To prepare the filling, beat the cream cheese and peanut butter, using an electric mixer. Add 1 cup of the powdered sugar and the butter. Beat until fluffy. In a separate bowl whip the cream until soft peaks form. Add the remaining 2 tablespoons powdered sugar and the vanilla and whip until stiff. Fold 1/4 of this into the peanut butter mixture. Fold in the remaining cream. Spoon the filling into the crust and chill a minimum of 3 hours.

To prepare the topping, bring the cream to a boil in a heavy saucepan. Add the chocolate and stir until smooth. Cool to lukewarm. Spread on the pie and chill for 2 more hours.
SERVES 8

Chef Richard Canestrari,
Café at Wexford

Crust:
1 cup graham cracker crumbs
1/4 cup sugar
1/2 stick butter, melted

Filling:
8 ounces cream cheese, softened
1 cup chunky peanut butter
1 cup + 2 tablespoons powdered sugar
1/4 stick butter
1/2 cup chilled whipping cream
1 tablespoon vanilla extract

Topping:
1/2 cup whipping cream
3/4 cup semi-sweet chocolate chips

Pears in Red Wine

4 medium smooth-
  skinned pears*
juice of 1 lemon
1/2 cup sugar
1 cup red wine
1 vanilla bean, split
  lengthwise
1 sprig fresh thyme
2 peppercorns
1 clove
4 tablespoons crème de
  cassis

*May substitute 8 very
small pears, unpeeled.

Peel, core and cut the pears in half. Place the pears in a pan just large enough to hold them. Add the remaining ingredients and cover. Bring to a boil. Reduce to a slow simmer for 30 minutes.

Lift the pears out and place in a bowl. Spoon the sauce over them. Baste occasionally.

Refrigerate overnight. Spoon the sauce over the pears again before serving.

SERVES 4

Chef Dave Plemmons,
Renaissance

Pecan Pie

Preheat the oven to 350°. Beat the eggs until light, adding the sugar gradually. Add the syrup, salt, vanilla , melted butter, and pecans. Pour the mixture into the shell. Bake approximately 60 minutes until the crust is light brown.
SERVES 8

3 eggs
1 cup dark brown
   sugar
1 cup light corn syrup
1/8 teaspoon salt
1 teaspoon vanilla
1 teaspoon melted
   butter
1 cup pecans,
   chopped
1, 9" pastry shell,
   uncooked

Chef Tom Oliva,
Crazy Crab, Harbour Town

1 Granny Smith apple
2 tablespoons sugar
2 tablespoons bread
  flour
1/4 teaspoon cinnamon
pinch of nutmeg
lemon juice to taste
1/4 stick butter, melted

Scalloped Apples

Quarter the apple and core. Do not peel. Slice it very thin and toss the slices with all of the other ingredients, except the butter. Heat a small sauté pan until hot. Add the butter and the apple mixture. Cook for 2 minutes until golden brown. Flip the apples like an egg, and cook an additional 2 minutes. Serve as a side order or as a main dish.

Serving suggestions: sprinkle with powdered sugar or a dollop of sour cream.

SERVES 1

Chef Sarah Bowman,
Hyatt Regency

Snowballs

Preheat the oven to 450°. Line a baking sheet with waxed paper.

Combine the almonds, 2 cups of sugar, 8 teaspoons of the egg white, and the chocolate chips. Work the ingredients into a firm dough which just binds together. Take heaped table-spoons of the mixture in your hands and roll about 25 small balls. Dip each into the remaining beaten egg whites, then coat with the remaining powdered sugar.

Bake on the prepared sheet for 2 minutes until crisp on the outside. Cool slightly. Transfer to a wire rack to cool completely.
SERVES 8-10

1 1/4 cups roasted almonds, chopped
3 cups powdered sugar, sifted
2 egg whites, lightly beaten with a fork
1/4 cup mini chocolate chips

Chef Ed Buffkin,
Swiss Pastry Shoppe

1/2 cup flour
1/2 cup cornstarch
1/2 cup water
1 egg
1/2 cup sugar
1/4 cup cinnamon
24 cleaned, fresh
    strawberries
3 cups oil
vanilla ice cream

Strawberries Supreme

Mix the first four ingredients to form a batter and set aside. Mix the sugar and cinnamon in a bowl and also set aside.

Dip the strawberries into the batter and fry for 2 minutes in the hot oil. Drain. While still hot, roll the fried berries in the sugar mixture. Serve immediately over ice cream.
SERVES 4

Chef Cynthia Hair,
Hyatt Regency

Swiss Chocolate Cookies

Preheat oven to 375°. Line several baking sheets with waxed paper. Put the butter and the sugar in a bowl and cream together until light and fluffy. Sift the hazelnuts and the flour together. Add to the creamed mixture, along with the almond extract and cinnamon. Beat to make a soft dough. Roll in waxed paper to form a cylinder 12" long and 2" around. Slice into 1/4" slices and bake until golden brown. Melt the chocolate. Stir in the melted butter and cool to room temperature. Spoon a little of the chocolate mixture between two of the cookies. Stick them together back to back and sprinkle them with powdered sugar.
YIELDS 20

1 stick unsalted butter, softened
1 cup powdered sugar, sifted
1 cup hazelnuts, roasted and ground
3/4 cup all-purpose flour
1/2 teaspoon almond extract
1/4 teaspoon cinnamon
1/2 cup Swiss chocolate
2 tablespoons sweet butter, melted

Chef Ed Buffkin,
Swiss Pastry Shoppe

Swiss Fruit Crumble

Fruit Crumble:
3 cups fresh
fruit (chopped
blackberries, apples,
plums, pitted
cherries)
2 1/3 cups sugar
3/4 cup all-purpose
flour
pinch of salt
4 tablespoons hard
unsalted butter
1/3 cup light brown
sugar

Custard Sauce:
2 1/2 cups milk
1/2 teaspoon vanilla
extract
1/4 teaspoon cinnamon
2 tablespoons sugar
4 egg yolks, beaten

Place the fruit in a buttered, oven-proof dish and add the white sugar.

To prepare the crumble, sift the flour and the salt together. Add the butter and rub by hand until the dough resembles lumpy bread crumbs. Stir in the brown sugar. Spoon the crumble over the fruit and bake in a 350° preheated oven until the top is browned. Serve with the custard sauce.

To prepare the custard sauce, gently heat the milk with the vanilla and cinnamon to just below the simmering point. Cover, remove from the heat and let sit 15 minutes. Blend the sugar and the egg yolks. Gradually stir in the milk. Heat gently, stirring constantly until the sauce thickens enough to coat a spoon.
SERVES 6 - 8

Chef Ed Buffkin,
Swiss Pastry Shoppe

Tiramisu

Sprinkle the sponge cake with 3 tablespoons of Kahlua. In a large bowl, whip the cream cheese until smooth. Mix in the powdered sugar. Slowly add the cream and beat until thickened. Add the rest of the Kahlua, the espresso and vanilla to the mixture. Beat until thick - approximately 1 minute. Spread the cream cheese mixture on top of the cake and dust with the cocoa powder, leaving the sides bare. Refrigerate for at least 2 hours.
YIELDS: 1 cake

chocolate sponge cake 10" round x 1 1/2" thick
1 pound and 2 ounces cream cheese
1 1/2 cups powdered sugar
3 cups heavy cream
3 tablespoons, plus 1/3 cup Kahlua
1/2 teaspoon espresso
1 teaspoon vanilla extract

Chef Anthony Mastropole,
Hyatt Regency

Tropical Cheesecake

1/3 cup sweet butter
1 3/4 cups Oreo
cookies, crushed
12 ounces cream
cheese, softened
2/3 cup sour cream
2/3 cup plain yogurt
1/2 cup sugar
3 eggs, separated
1 tablespoon plus 1
teaspoon unflavored
gelatin
2 tablespoons water
2/3 cup whipping
cream, whipped
1 pound assorted fresh
fruit
apricot jelly

To prepare the crust, grease an 8" springform pan. Melt the butter in a small pan on low heat. Stir in the crushed Oreo cookies. Press into the greased pan. Set aside.

To prepare the filling, beat the cream cheese, sour cream, yogurt, 1/4 cup plus 2 tablespoons of sugar and the egg yolks until smooth. Combine the gelatin and the water in a small pan. Simmer to dissove the gelatin. Stir into the cheese mixture. Fold the whipped cream into the cheese mixture. Beat the egg whites with the remaining sugar until soft peaks form and fold into the cheese mixture. Spoon the filling into the prepared crust. Chill 2 to 3 hours until set.

Garnish with cut fruit arranged on the cheese cake. Brush with 1/4 cup melted apricot jelly.
SERVES 8-10

Chef Ed Buffkin,
Swiss Pastry Shoppe

White Chocolate Mousse

Chop the chocolate into small pieces. Heat the cream to boiling point, but do not boil. Pour the hot cream over the chocolate. Whisk until the chocolate is melted. Next, whisk in the butter, then the egg yolks. Whip the egg whites, gradually adding sugar to form a meringue. Fold the meringue into the chocolate mixture. Pour into serving dishes. Refrigerate for 3 hours before serving. SERVES 6 - 8

1 pound white chocolate
1 cup whipping cream
3/4 cup butter, room temperature
12 eggs, separated
8 teaspoons sugar

Chef Thierry Saglier,
Harbour Lights Bakery

Crust:
1 1/4 cups ground
  shortbread cookies
1/4 cup almonds, ground
2 tablespoons sugar
1/8 teaspoon almond
  extract
3 tablespoons unsalted
  butter, melted

Filling:
3/4 cup white
  chocolate, finely
  chopped
24 ounces cream
  cheese, softened
1 cup Neufchatel
  cheese, softened
5 large eggs, room
  temperature
3/4 cup sugar
3 tablespoons flour
1 teaspoon vanilla
  extract
1/4 teaspoon almond
  extract

1 pint raspberries

White Chocolate Raspberry Cheesecake

Preheat oven to 350°. Mix the first four ingredients. Blend enough of the butter in to bind. Press firmly to the bottom of a 10" springform pan. Bake for 10 minutes. Cool on a rack. Reduce oven to 325°. Melt the chocolate in a double boiler, stirring until smooth. Cool.

Beat the cheeses until smooth. Blend in the eggs, one at a time. Add the sugar, flour, vanilla and almond extract and mix. Stir 1 cup of the mixture into the warm white chocolate. Mix into the remaining filling in the bowl. Pour over the crust. Bake for 40 minutes, until the cheesecake has firm edges but center still wiggles. Cool on a rack. Cover and refrigerate overnight.

Serve garnished with the raspberries.
SERVES 12 - 15

Chef Deborah Van Plew,
Flamingo's Café

Glossary

BASES
All bases used in this book are Minor's products and can be found in most grocery stores. They come in a variety of seafood flavors, which include clam, crab, lobster and shrimp.

BOUQUET GARNI
Herbs tied together or wrapped in cheesecloth (parsley, thyme and a bayleaf) used to flavor soups, stews and broths.

CARPACCIO
An Italian dish consisting of thin shavings of raw beef, or fish.

CHANTERELLE
A wild mushroom with a nutty, sometimes fruity flavor. Can be found dried or canned in many supermarkets. Known to grow in the Pacific Northwest and East Coast, but mostly imported from Europe.

CHERVIL
A member of the parsley family with a mild flavor. Also called cicily and sweet cicily.

CHEVRE CHEESE
A pure white, goatsmilk cheese with a tart flavor. Chèvre is French for "goat." Included are Bucheron and Montrachet. "Pur Chèvre" ensures that the cheese is made entirely from goat's milk; if this designation is not on the label, it may have the addition of cows milk.

CLARIFIED BUTTER

Unsalted butter very slowly melted. This allows the milk solids to separate and sink to the bottom. What is left is clear or "clarified" butter with a higher smoking point which can be used to cook at higher temperatures.

COBIA

For information on this or any other fish or shellfish, call the US Government Hotline at 1-800-332-4010.

COULIS

A thick purée or sauce.

COURT BOUILLON

A broth made by cooking various herbs and vegetables in water for about 30 minutes. These usually include an onion studded with cloves, celery, carrots and a bouquet garni.

CORNICHON

French for "gherkin," cornichons are crisp, tart pickes made from tiny gherkin cucumbers.

DEGLAZE

This is done by heating a small amount of liquid (usually wine or stock) in the bottom of a pan after the food and excess fat have been removed, to loosen the browned bits of food which becomes the base for a sauce to be used on the food prepared in the pan.

DEMI-GLACE

A combination of beef stock, madeira or sherry and tomato paste, reduced by half. A nice brown gravy will also work well in a pinch.

FISH HOTLINE
For more information, call 1-800-332-4010.

FLUTED
A grooved pattern in certain fruits and vegetables strictly for show.

JULIENNE
Thin, matchstick cuts of food such as carrots or potatoes. Often used as a garnish.

NEUFCHATEL CHEESE
The French, original version of American cream cheese.

OLD BAY® SEASONING
A seafood spice, made by McCormick spices, available in most grocery stores. Call 1-800-632-5847 for more information.

PAPILLOTE
The French term for paper frills used to decorate tips of rib bones, such as those on Crown Roasts. 'En Papillote' refers to food baked inside of greased parchment paper.

PERNOD
A licorice-flavored liqueur similar to absinthe.

RADICCHIO
A red-leafed Italian chicory often used as a salad green. The most common varieties used in the US are Verona and Treviso.

RED SWISS CHARD
Also called ruby chard, a member of the beet family grown for its tender greens and crisp stalks.

ROUX
A mixture, usually equal parts of flour and butter, cooked slowly over a low heat, used to thicken sauces, gravies and soups or stews.

STILTON
One of the finest English blue cheeses. Made from whole cows' milk.

TERRINE
A container used for cooking patés.

USDA MEAT & POULTRY HOTLINE
For more information, call 1-800-535-4555.

WAHOO
Similar to Albacore, the Wahoo is a slightly sweet, fine, white fish. Usually baked, broiled or grilled.

WATER BATH
The process of cooking food by placing it in a container in a large, shallow pan of warm water which surrounds the food with gentle heat.

Index

ORDER FORMS

Use the order forms below
for obtaining additional copies of this cookbook.

Mail to:
The Chefs of Hilton Head
Southern Islands Publishing
PO Box 69
Beaufort, SC 29901

Please send me _____ copies of The Chefs of Hilton Head at $11.95, plus $1.75 postage and handling. S.C. residents add 5% sales tax.
Enclosed is my check or money order for $_____________

Name _________________________________
Address _______________________________
City, State, Zip _________________________

Please send me _____ copies of The Chefs of Hilton Head at $11.95, plus $1.75 postage and handling. S.C. residents add 5% sales tax.
Enclosed is my check or money order for $_____________

Name _________________________________
Address _______________________________
City, State, Zip _________________________